"D U M M Y"
HANSON

A DEAF BASEBALL PITCHER'S LIFE
IN THE HEARING WORLD

by Jim Johnson

Beaver's Pond Press, Inc.

ISBN 10: 1-59298-256-5
ISBN 13: 978-1-59298-256-1

Library of Congress Catalog Number: 2008933814

Printed in the United States of America

First Printing: 2008

12 11 10 09 08   5 4 3 2 1

Cover and interior design by James Monroe Design, LLC.

Beaver's Pond Press, Inc.

Beaver's Pond Press, Inc.
7104 Ohms Lane, Suite 101
Edina, MN 55439–2129
(952) 829-8818
www.BeaversPondPress.com

to order, visit www.BookHouseFulfillment.com
or call 1-800-901-3480. Reseller discounts available.

Dedicated to the memories of my grandfather, Henry Johnson,
and his son, my father, Harlow V. Johnson—both baseballists.
They taught me how to keep my eye on the ball.

CONTENTS

CONTENTS

FOREWORD

The Minnesota State Academy for the Deaf (MSAD) has been home to more than 4,000 deaf and hard of hearing children since 1863. In the late 1800s, Esten Hanson, as a young boy, attended the deaf school.

Esten was a typical student with a special talent and interest in baseball. In that regard, he was actually not unusual, as sports activities and competition with neighboring schools has always been an important part of the school's history. Students at the school were excited and supported their teams—teams and activities that kept students active and healthy. During winter, the games and competition provided incentives to get in shape and be prepared for upcoming spring events. At one time, showing great ingenuity, even though they had to suffer with cold hands, the students unraveled their mittens to make baseballs when their ball supply was lacking.

Sports activities at MSAD continue to be important. Alumni return annually for homecoming weekend as avid spectators, when current teams play football and volleyball games. Alumni return also to see their former classmates and close friends who grew up with them at the deaf school, which had become their second home. As with Esten, friendships formed at the school often last a lifetime.

MSAD Superintendent Noyes was a devout Christian, which explains the origin of the sign "chapel" that alumni use when describing Noyes Hall Auditorium. They use this sign because that is where Superintendent Noyes preached to the children daily. He felt strongly that the children needed to learn about God. Though the separation of church and state prevents any further preaching of Christianity, the sign "chapel" is still used to describe Noyes Hall Auditorium.

As the current superintendent, I find it interesting that one challenge for the superintendent during Esten's time was in having to explain to the public that the school was in fact a school, not an institution. This is the same message we communicate today: MSAD is a school, a special school for deaf children; it is a boarding school, not an institution. Children attend school classes, study academics, and participate in recreational activities and athletics, the same as children attending public or private school.

After Esten left the deaf school and his baseball-playing days continued, newspapers wrote about his deafness almost like it was an advantage. They suggested his concentration might be better because he couldn't hear hecklers. They never acknowledged his hearing loss as a possible explanation for an outfield collision with a teammate when he obviously couldn't hear or call off a fly ball.

Did Esten have a sense of humor? Did he fall in love? What might he have done after his baseball playing days were over had his life not been cut short? Jim has given us a gift, a glimpse at the life of one of our alumni and a taste of the rich history of the Minnesota State Academy for the Deaf.

—Linda Mitchell, Superintendent, Minnesota State Academy for the Deaf,
Faribault, Minnesota. February 2008

PREFACE

The seeds of Esten "Dummy" Hanson were planted more than seventy years ago when I, as a small boy, asked my grandfather, "What kind of a pitcher was Dummy Hanson?" and "Was he any good?" His answer was, as I remember it, "Dummy was a fine pitcher, a real crackerjack!"

In April 2001, I wrote in my column "Thoughts While Thinking" in *The Kerkhoven Banner*, an account of the baseball 1904 encounter between the visiting Boston Bloomers and the Kerkhoven team, accompanied by photographs of both teams. About a month later, Verna Johnson Gomer informed me that "Dummy" Hanson shown in the team picture, was her uncle. Furthermore, she added, we were related by marriage!

On May 31, *The Kerkhoven Banner* published my follow-up article, which recounted Esten Hanson's baseball experience in Kerkhoven during the 1903 and 1904 seasons, as culled from that newspaper's game reports. When I wrote the article, it was my belief that his talents as a baseball player were exclusively those of a pitcher and that his baseball career was brief.

Giving the matter no further thought, and satisfied that I had exhausted the subject of Esten Hanson, I was able to put him behind me for a few weeks. But then I began wondering. *What would it have been like being deaf and playing baseball? What was a deaf person's education like in the 1800s? How would Esten have gotten started in baseball? How would the teams handle the many practical on-the-field problems, like how to signal each other or how to call for catching a fly ball?*

This book is the result of my research into this unique man's life.

It would not have been possible to trace Esten's footsteps without the assistance of many, many individuals, including those with personal knowledge of Esten Hanson's history: professional employees of state historical societies; elected county officials; municipal employees; librarians; directors; volunteers of county historical societies; and the administration, faculty, staff, and present and former students of the Minnesota State Academy for the Deaf in Faribault, Minnesota.

I would be remiss without expressing appreciation and individually recognizing those people who accompanied me during the entire journey.

Verna Johnson Gomer, daughter of one of Esten's sisters, jump-started this book by telling me, "He was my uncle." She has wholeheartedly and without reservation provided information through personal interviews, written correspondence, emails, telephone conversations, and photographs of Esten Hanson.

Vivian Hanson Nelson, the daughter of Esten's brother, Bernt, shared her personal knowledge of her grandparents' immediate family. In one instance, for example, she identified a man sitting next to Esten as a sibling, who through sign language often interpreted for him.

Audrey Kvam Wendland's *The Hanson Family* served as a road map to Esten's family. Wendland has been a source of encouragement.

Lola Brand, administrative assistant to the superintendent of MSAD, American Sign Language interpreter, keeper of the key to the MSAD museum, and arranger of personal interviews, was endowed with the quality of patience.

Mike Cashman and Dave Olson taught me how to talk with a deaf person.

Robert and Myrtice Gordhamer, the son and daughter-in-law of Oliver "Happy" Gordhamer, Esten's catcher, were long-time friends who shared memories of Happy's baseball days, and trustingly made available original heirloom photographs of the Kerkhoven ball team.

Gregory Salmers, MLS, librarian for the Estevan Public Library Branch, and branch supervisor for the Southeast Regional Library, Estevan, Saskatchewan, Canada, determined the availability of baseball records, including archival material in Regina, Canada. For the most part, his work resulted in negative answers, but, nonetheless, he answered questions put to him. His enthusiasm was most welcome while investigating Esten's Canadian experience.

Gregory M. Wysk, reference specialist, State Historical Society of North Dakota, responded to my many email inquiries. If the question was beyond his area of expertise, he unhesitatingly referred me to the appropriate specialist. He was my North Dakota expert.

Sarah Scholl, North Dakota Department of Health, Division of Vital Records, not only produced a certified copy of Esten's death certificate, but also took the extra step of locating his obituary in a 1908 issue of the *McVille Journal*. The latter revealed Esten's popularity in that village, and the fact that, eyesight permitting, he occasionally worked for the newspaper, indicating he had not forsaken his deaf school training as a printer.

The Minnesota Historical Society reference librarians observed, assisted, directed, and offered their personal and professional support for seven years while I searched and printed microfilm archival material. I am most grateful to them for always having time for me: Ruth Bauer Anderson, Nick Duncan, Debbie Miller, Steve Nielsen, Kathryn Otto, Hampton Smith, Duane P. Swanson, Lisa Whitehill, and Jane Wong.

I also thank Marlys Gallagher, director, Swift County Historical Society in Benson, Minnesota; Mona Nelson-Balcer, director, Kandiyohi County Historical Society in Willmar, Minnesota; Otter Tail County Historical Society in Fergus Falls, Minnesota; and Pioneer Library in New London and Spicer, Minnesota—and their staffs.

Renae Arneson, city auditor, McVille, North Dakota, always, and without exception, responded to my emails and calls seeking information about her city's early days. She also made available several commemorative publications tracing McVille's history.

Additional thanks go to the Oregon Area Historical Museum, Oregon, Wisconsin, specifically Melanie Woodworth, who was instrumental in obtaining copies of original photographs documenting the Boston Bloomer's 1908 appearance in that city, which echoed descriptions by *The Kerkhoven Banner* when that team made a stop there in 1904. The originals were thoughtfully made available by their owner, Florine Paulson, for reproduction purposes.

Patricia A. Kytola, director, Minnesota Transportation Museum; Nick Modders, chairman, Board of Directors, Minnesota Transportation Museum; and John Thomas, custodian of records, Great Northern Railway Historical Society, St. Paul, Minnesota, also provided help. This book was professionally, and cooperatively, edited by April Michelle Davis.

Finally, Marilynn L. Johnson, with whom I entered into a nuptial agreement more than fifty years ago—how does one properly credit my best friend for her contributions to "Dummy"?

INTRODUCTION

Over the centuries, the many thousands of accomplished deaf people that have contributed to American culture have been viewed primarily as "deaf" contributors, rather than as American. Dummy Hanson also could have been consigned to this fate: unknown to posterity, nondescript, and another notable deaf person not receiving due acknowledgment. But given the context of nineteenth-century America, Dummy Hanson lived an extraordinary life, worthy of final review by all Americans. Of utmost importance, his deafness never created any insurmountable barriers for him. In some way, this historical examination will show his example for others, deaf or not, to follow.

CHAPTER ONE

MINNESOTA SCHOOL FOR THE DEAF

In 1858, the year Minnesota became the nation's thirty-second state, the Minnesota Legislature decided to locate "a deaf and dumb asylum" in Faribault, a town in south-central Minnesota. Though the asylum was initially only meant to be a place to house these "so-afflicted" people, two years later, the legislature provided $1,500 to establish an educational program for "blind and deaf mutes."

R. M. Kinney and his wife became the school's first official superintendent and matron in 1863, hired away from the Ohio School for the Deaf by Faribault attorney Rodney Mott, a commissioner of the new school.

From his first minute in Minnesota, Superintendent Kinney was an enthusiastic advocate. Appealing to the commissioners only days before Christmas 1863, and aware his words were being recorded for the legislature, Superintendent Kinney seized on a unique opportunity to educate. What he expressed framed the parochial world Esten Hanson would enter twenty-four years later. In his speech, Kinney said:

It was supposed for centuries that the deaf and dumb could never be reached by any art, nor improved by any wisdom or care; and it occurred to no one, that written words could possibly represent ideas to those who knew nothing of their sounds. The first instance of a deaf mute who had learned to write, of whom there is any account, was sometime in the fourteenth century. Jerome Cardan, an Italian philosopher, during the fifteenth century, was the first to affirm the possibility of educating the deaf and dumb.

The condition and prospects of this unfortunate class were wretched beyond conception. Parents considered it a disgrace to have such offspring; they took great pains to conceal them from the eyes of the world, and supposed they had discharged their whole duty to them, by merely supplying their animal wants. In some countries they were regarded as monsters and deprived of life as soon as the misfortune was known. If their lives were spared, they were, in the eyes of men and the law, idiots. There has been a great change in the estimation in which they are held, owing to the transforming power of the Bible ... but remaining uneducated, the deaf mute is still an outcast from society, shut out from the blessings of social life, and the means of mental and moral improvement.

Deaf mutes are imitative animals, exhibiting but slight

indications of intellect and moral character. The dim consciousness of right and wrong which they possess, they learn by experience. Observation teaches them that virtuous actions are approved, and that vicious ones are punished. The extent to which this experience will influence them, depends upon their early associations and natural temperament. Their animal natures develop themselves, like spontaneous combustion; but no latent heat cherishes and stimulates the germs of intellect, or of the nobler powers of their souls. Their bodies grow, it may be, until they are giants, but their minds are still in swaddling clothes.

Some theologians hold fast to the dogma, that in all men the idea of God is innate. This is not so very strange, when we consider that it has been relied upon as an argument against infidels for centuries. It looks like a concession to the enemy to give it up. But it is always better to meet a fact fairly, than to evade or deny it. The practical experience of every teacher of deaf mutes certainly shows the fallacy of the doctrine. The idea of God is one that the deaf and dumb, uneducated and unaided by friends, never originate. It presupposes a degree of mental development to which they never attain.

Many educated deaf mutes, at different times, for more than forty years, have been questioned in regard to their knowledge of God; origin of men and animals; existence of their own souls, and notions concerning death, and the following are some of their replies:

'I had no notion of a God at all.'

'I had no idea of the beginning of the world, nor of the beings it contains.'

'I thought it was strange that man should die. I felt that it was melancholy and terrible. I thought that death was an eternal sleep like that of the beasts.'

Thus it appears that the darkness in which the deaf and dumb are enveloped is so profound, that they have no inheritance in this common birthright of other men. They may be surrounded by sympathizing friends; by civilizing, enlightening and Christianizing influences; they may be literally bathed in light, but the isolation of their minds is still complete.

There must be some connection between their minds and the minds of others. In no other way can their intellectual powers be developed. This connection is *language*, which is the key that sets at large their solitary souls, and permits them to look forth upon the hitherto unintelligible world. Though it be observed, it only helps them across the threshold of the prison house of ignorance, where they must be met by friends who will robe them with their sympathy and love.

They must become members of an Institution where ample provisions are made for their education; where teachers skilled in the use of signs, and really desiring their good, are willing to perform the labor of Missionaries, and where moral force still, deep and powerful, is brought to bear upon them. Light and heat change leaf buds into flowers; so do these men qualified by years of experience, impart warmth to the germ of thought and feeling, stimulating its vitality so long dormant, and increasing little by little the internal force of their pupils' minds, until they are liberated from their winding sheets of silence and ignorance.

When deaf mutes enter an Institution, they begin at once to appreciate the enjoyments of social life. They are so active and cheerful that no one would suppose that the hand of misfortune bore heavily upon them. They are no longer unhappy. Their eyes brighten with intelligence. Their faces are radiant with a new-born light. Kind hands have broken the spell that held them by its nightmare influence. Their souls have waked up, not in paroxysms of fear, hopelessly struggling for relief, but with a strange rush of happiness thrilling their hearts. No wild screams of delight fill the air, no words are spoken but their souls vibrate the joys such as Lazarus felt when he stepped forth from the gloom of the grave; or such as the deaf man experienced, when his ears were unstopped by one, 'who came to charm trembling souls with the whisper of peace inspiring compassion.' A beautiful light flashes upon the mysteries of their being, opening regions of thought, all unexplored and at once excites inquiries. They learn to *think*, which next to joys of sanctified hearts, is the greatest blessing that could be conferred upon them.

Knowledge is worth but little without some means of expressing it. By close application, written language may be so acquired as to bring them into intimate communion with men.

Those persons who regard labor in this department as uninteresting and unproductive of important results, may well bestow some special attention upon this subject. They may be friends of the deaf and dumb in theory, and acknowledge the utility of instructing them; but their cold intellectual assent is worth nothing, so long as their

sympathies and love are not enlisted; for their hearts can
see much farther, and urge to much more efficient labor
than their heads.

Two months after the Battle of Gettysburg, in September 1863,
deaf students between the ages of ten and twenty-five enrolled in
Faribault free of charge on the first day of school; but they had to
be in good health, of sound mind, and free of contagious diseases.
They supplied their own clothing and a trunk, and a small sum was
deposited with the superintendent for shoe repair and other
expenses. School began the second Wednesday in September and
ended in June. The course of instruction, initially, for most
students was five years, and for slow learners, seven. Kinney, fired
up seeing progress in students his first year, aggressively sought
more. The stay would be lengthened by the time Esten enrolled.

Commissioner Mott, by then Judge Mott, recalled on the
school's twenty-fifth anniversary celebration in 1888 that the
school had, on the first day in 1863, "eight desolate, homesick
pupils, who had no idea whether they were consigned to a perpetual
prison or were brought here to be fattened for the market." They
had classes in the former home of Major Fowler on Front Street in
Faribault. Some students refused the first few days to eat along with
the others, and these Mott invited to his home, where he offered
"pats on the head" and other signs suggesting friendship to help
relieve anxiety. (In 1888, the year after Esten began, the school
had 175 students.)

Kinney wrote in his first report to the legislature:

[The students] really feel religious obligation and desire
the approval of God. This susceptibility, which is an interesting characteristic, suggests the highest motives for right

action in life, and makes it comparatively easy to control them. God has not left the deaf and dumb without language but he has kindly supplied a natural, universal and powerful language of signs, and they spontaneously resort to it as a means of holding communion with those about them.

If children had never heard spoken language, it is quite certain that they would not themselves speak; but is equally certain that they would be able to express their wants and various states of feeling, through the medium of signs, to any people, whether savage or civilized. A look, calm as a summer evening; a smile, like the play of sunlight over a beautiful landscape; and an eye beaming with pleasure, as well as the threatening scowl, the flashing eye, and defiant bearing, is language, universal and powerful.

Replacing the retiring Kinney in 1866, school commissioners hired Dr. Jonathan Noyes from the school for the deaf in Philadelphia. Noyes bore an authoritative face and a bushy mustache and ran off of nervous energy. People considered him benevolent and firm. Originally destined for the ministry, Noyes earned his education at Phillip's Academy and Yale College. He was a hearing person and was Esten's superintendent, presiding over the school officially until 1896. Noyes faithfully continued the moral groundwork laid by Kinney and would be one of Esten's male mentors.

CHAPTER TWO

THE HANSONS

Tosten Sagedalen Hanson emigrated from Norway with his parents in 1852, to what is now south-central Minnesota, near the town of Faribault, then part of Minnesota Territory. Shortly after Minnesota became a state in 1858, Berit (Betsy) Bonde came with her family, also settling near Faribault, in 1864.

By 1867, Tosten and Betsy Hanson were married, and immediately moved to the prairies of western Minnesota, settling down on a eighty-acre homestead in Swift County only a mile from the site of the Monson Lake Massacre, part of the 1862 Sioux Uprising.

The Hansons were isolated as any pioneer family would be. Three miles away, the hamlet of Sunburg wouldn't even boast a general store until 1879. Benson and its 400 citizens were twenty miles west, and Brooten, twenty miles north. New London was fifteen miles east. Kerkhoven was eleven miles south. Literally, the Hansons occupied the middle ground of what could be called nowhere.

In 1868, the Hansons had their first child, Isabelle. Betsy would have ten children. The living children would include Isabelle, Hans, Sarah, Caroline, Esten, Bernt, Julius, Ida, and Oline.

The Hansons had a pioneer lifestyle and lived within several miles of six families related by blood or marriage.

The family developed a resiliency necessary for sheer survival. In the summer of 1876, for example, the year before Esten's birth, a grasshopper swarm of biblical proportions destroyed all of the crops and vegetation in the area, including those on the Hanson farm. The grasshoppers laid their eggs and then left. A concerned Governor Pillsbury visited the devastation. In time, the legislature sent each farmer in the region $21.70, or the equivalent in wheat and peas, for seeding purposes.

In April 1877, with Betsy three months pregnant with Esten, a devastating fire nearly wiped out the village of Kerkhoven where the Hansons did most of their trading. Only a few structures survived, including the grain warehouse, two stores, and the train depot. As the Hansons and others were still dealing with this tragedy, two months later grasshoppers reappeared when eggs laid the previous year hatched. While many people fought the grass-hoppers with all means, local ministers seized the opportunity to preach repentance from sin. Perhaps the prayers worked, as suddenly, on July 10, the grasshopper swarms disappeared, completely and miraculously.

With all of these calamities, four young children, and a preg-nant wife, Tosten, who spoke little English, had plenty to worry about prior to Esten's birth.

Betsy gave birth to the fifth child, Esten, on October 15, 1877, and he was baptized into the Lutheran faith on November 4.

When he was born, Esten had the same babbling and sensor motor development as any other infant. He responded to touch; his eyes tracked movement. It shocked Betsy and Tosten upon learning of their son's almost total deafness. Given the culture of the time and the limited resources of pioneer life, they did not have any hope that their son could live a productive life, unless he had special schooling. But the educational tools necessary for the Hansons to teach a deaf child effectively did not exist in rural Minnesota.

However, they did raise him in a fun-loving, harmonious home that valued writing, reading, and speaking English. The children learned English at school and in time taught their mom and dad. One of Esten's sisters, Ida, went to the normal school to become a teacher. They especially enjoyed ethnic Norwegian music, and several of the children learned to play musical instruments. Betsy even smoked a corn-cob pipe, not an uncommon habit among pioneer women. Also, as a whole, they were an athletic and sports-loving family. Although unable to hear, as a boy running for a ball, Esten could feel the grass under his feet, the sunshine on his face, and the breeze on his back. Sports was an arena in which he could compete with the other boys.

Vivian Hanson Nelson, a daughter of Esten's brother, Bernt, said in a personal interview with the author that Esten could walk the distance from the house to the barn on his hands. Audrey Kvam Wendland, quoting a Hanson family friend, said, "Hilde-gard wrote that she has good memories of the Hanson/Sagedal families. She said they were witty, fun-loving, musical and positive-thinking. They seemed to take life in stride and could make the best of everything."

As Esten matured, he learned to tug on people's clothing to catch their attention and point at objects he wanted to have. He could speak only a few words: Mama, Papa, A, and B. The only sounds he heard were thunder and church bells. At home, he couldn't learn lip-reading because his family spoke two languages, English and Norwegian, meaning each object had two words and pronunciations.

Like modern-day parents of deaf children, Tosten and Betsy no doubt felt frustrated and even helpless at times when unable to communicate effectively. Given the cultural context, at some level, they probably also felt shame for bearing a deaf child, and later, guilt, for being unable to teach him. As with any child, Esten required attention, but the industrious and overworked Hansons didn't have much extra to share.

CHAPTER THREE

LIFE ON THE FARM

A public school was established in 1873 just two miles from the Hanson farm, which Esten Hanson's siblings attended, most likely getting there by foot. Esten never attended, which contributed to his having an immature knowledge of the world. The newspaper was published twenty miles away in Benson, and was in English, so the Hanson parents wouldn't have been able to explain much of it to Esten. Their primary news sources were the nuggets harvested from Sunday church fellowship and from neighbors or passing strangers.

At home, Esten used nonverbal communication and hand motions—a unique language only his family understood. His learning early in life consisted almost entirely of shadowing his father, mother, and siblings, and they talked for him when dealing with hearing persons outside the family. He helped his father harvest wood using a horse-drawn wagon (and a sled in winter) near Camp Lake and Norway Lake. Preparation for winter included banking the outside of the home with hay or manure to prevent drafts. Esten's jobs were to hand-carry firewood to the stove and water from a nearby well. Besides food prepared from their own harvest of wheat, and vegetables grown in the garden, the Hansons stocked their table with geese, duck, and fish from Norway Lake. Esten learned to trap muskrat, mink, and beaver, and they sold the furs for cash.

Taking care of basic needs also was more difficult. Water for bathing would have to be hauled and heated, outhouses and chamber pots would have to suffice for bodily functions—and an outhouse with a frosted-up seat did not invite dawdling. All of these activities were accomplished without electricity.

On Sundays, his family, dressed in their best, traveled to West Norway Lake Church, where a church bell rang, one of the few sounds Esten could hear. From the solemn expressions and hand motions to be still, he assumed something important was going on. A black-robed man spoke, gestured, gazed at the ceiling, and often stared into the attentive eyes of parishioners sitting in the pews. As Tosten and Betsy listened, they had just enough faith in a Sovereign God who could reach into their son's heart and faith in a school that could teach him. They and their Norwegian Lutheran friends prayed about his future.

Sometime prior to 1885, the Hansons took Esten to visit doctors in Glenwood, about twenty-five miles away, a day's trip by horse and buggy. Norwegian-born and licensed in Minnesota, the doctors offered no cure. Esten had congenital deafness, said the doctors—other common causes of deafness at the time were contagious diseases such as scarlet fever, cerebrospinal meningitis, brain fever, typhoid fever, and measles.

The 1885 Minnesota Census listed Esten, describing him as "deaf and dumb."

Having lived near Faribault prior to settling in Swift County, Tosten and Betsy Hanson more than likely had known of the existence of the School for the Deaf. If not, they knew neighbors had enrolled their daughter in 1886 at the school.

If the School for the Deaf admitted Esten, the nine-year-old boy would have to travel by rail to a school 165 miles away. But Betsy and Tosten felt they had no other alternative.

The Hansons, employing the help of an English-speaking friend, wrote a letter of inquiry to the School for the Deaf in spring 1887, and soon, Superintendent Noyes replied, including an application.

Faribault had become the center for educating those who did not fit the mold of society. The Minnesota Legislature had just that year renamed the Minnesota Deaf, Dumb and Blind Institute as the "Minnesota Institute for Defectives." The institute consisted of three departments: the Minnesota School for the Deaf, Minnesota School for the Blind, and Minnesota School for the Feeble-Minded. Each of the schools had its own campus and governance. Much to Noyes' relief, the newspapers, at least, no longer referred to the school as an "asylum," but he still regularly had to correct visitors who used the term or called it "public charity."

Betsy may have wept after receiving Esten's official acceptance letter. She would have to push her young son from the nest without being able to warn or prepare him sufficiently, except what little they could communicate by use of hand signals.

CHAPTER FOUR

ON TO FARIBAULT

Leading up to the departure of Esten to the Minnesota Institute for the Defectives, Tosten and Betsy experienced an avalanche of emotion. After all, Gena Torkelson, a local deaf girl, had ventured off to the School for the Deaf a year before but had passed away from typhoid pneumonia. Her death broke the Torkelsons' hearts.

Esten was friendly, free-spirited, and had an easy smile—his natural temperament adjusted remarkably well to change. At the School for the Deaf, he could learn skills like reading, writing, lip-reading, and signing; he could learn a trade so that he could become independent, and he could be with other deaf boys and girls. But would he be the same personable Esten at his return in June? Would he pick up unhealthy habits or bad morals? At the same time, the family had the ever-present necessity of caring for its six other children, including three under the age of six. With the children, farm work, and the rigors of everyday life, they wouldn't have that much free time to engage in worrying. Daily life around the Hanson home would be vastly different, though, in the sense that Esten wouldn't be near the top of everyone's list of daily concerns.

The departure day for Esten was September 14, 1887. He boarded No. 10 of the St. Paul, Minneapolis & Manitoba Railway in Kerkhoven at 2:25 a.m.

As the engine entering Kerkhoven coughed black-coal clouds, it produced a grotesque silhouette on the moonlit western skyline. The train wheels clacked, and an uncomfortable knot of anxiety formed in Betsy's stomach. Esten clutched her hand at the sight of the train. Out on the track, the depot agent waved his lantern, signaling the engineer of No. 10 that there was an early-morning passenger. The train road up the slight incline to the station and then crawled to a hissing halt.

When the brakes hissed, Esten heard nothing. The depot agent shepherded him and his trunk onto the waiting train and motioned at him with palms down, instructing him to stay seated. As soon as the agent departed, Esten pressed his eyes up against the window, and blurted, "Mama" and "Papa." Tears rolled off his cheeks. His mother wept quietly into a cotton handkerchief, while his father bit at his lower lip, an uncharacteristic display of emotion. As his parents instinctively moved toward the train, his mother forced a reassuring smile, and Esten blinked. Suddenly, Betsy Hanson's sadness began softening. She reminded herself that the deaf school just might be able to teach Esten the Christian faith, provide a solid education, and coach him in a trade—everything she couldn't.

Esten kept his parents in view as long as he could, until finally he slumped defeatedly onto his hard seat, wondering if he would ever see them again. Through what he had learned from his sister, he would be traveling to the school where Gena Torkelson died. Was he off to his death, too?

As the train rumbled along, Esten noticed other children in the gloomy passenger coach. Watching Esten board that morning were eight-year-old George Corbett of Clay County; fifteen-year-old Katie Galvin; thirteen-year-old Oscar Gaarder; and twenty-one-year-old Arsidas Benoit, deaf at age sixteen, from Benson. Thirty minutes from Kerkhoven, the train reached the depot in sleepy Willmar and picked up the fourteen-year-old dressmaking student Pauline Peterson, who had begun taking this annual railroad trip in 1881. The train later gathered four older deaf boys at stops in Meeker and Wright counties. As each new deaf student boarded, Esten gained a degree of confidence. Soon after the sun rose above a horizon of oak and maple, the train arrived in bustling Minneapolis at 6:55 a.m.

Single-filing off the dusty rail car, the students banded together. Esten was just one of 175 Minnesota boys and girls expected at Faribault, and one of thirty new students that year. Pauline Peterson and Katie Galvin, who had taken the trip a number of times and were the only female students on board, perhaps put reassuring arms around the shoulders of the two younger boys, George and Esten. The boys followed the girls and met one of the teachers, who escorted them to the Milwaukee Depot, a four-block walk, to catch the next train.

Outside, Minneapolis was alive in magical motion, powered by the activity of thousands of energetic residents. It was unfathomably bigger than Benson: fancy carriages in the streets, shop owners hurriedly walking about, the familiar scent of horse manure (but much more of it); storefront windows brimming with housewares, baskets of produce. Katie and Pauline pointed out the Mississippi River, giant grain mills, and colossal buildings. Throughout the day, more groups of deaf children arrived at the depot. Similar scenes occurred at depots in St. Paul, Owatonna, and Austin, Minnesota. With all the groups, the convergence point, by dinner time, would be the School for the Deaf in Faribault, a large town of 6,000 people, 70 miles south (two hours by train) of Minneapolis.

Esten, though dreadfully tired, conjured up enough boyish energy that evening to be wide-eyed and ecstatic, as he saw the Minnesota School for the Deaf for the first time. After passing through a wide gate on an imposing hill, and onto the oak-shaded campus, he could see all of the large buildings.

The dome of Mott Hall towered above its four floors and two colossal wings to kiss the Minnesota sky. The top of the flagpole that thrusted skyward from the dome was 150 feet off the ground. From Esten's viewpoint, a stretch of bare ground—where a pond had been only weeks before—stood between him and the building, accentuating the grand structure's oddity. The building probably contained more lumber, window glass, doorknobs, staircases, pillows, and beds than all of Kerkhoven's rough-cut homes combined. The central portion of Mott Hall housed classrooms, administrative offices, and residential facilities for staff members, including the superintendent and his family. The wings served as dormitories. The building had central steam heating, and a covered passageway joining the wings in the rear housed a bowling alley. Esten slept that first night in a sea of boys and beds.

The Minnesota School for the Deaf occupied a twenty-acre bluff overlooking the Straight River and Faribault, where, "Our mute wards whose only avenue of knowledge is the eye" would have sight of the busy world "without the evil effects of actual contact therewith," wrote R. M. Kinney. He had worked hard to keep the campus safe and secure, away from the city's sins, and he had set aside ample room for vegetable plots and fruit trees for a hungry and growing student body. Superintendent Noyes, in addition, was especially concerned about student safety, particularly when students were permitted to walk to Faribault shops and entertainment. Deaf pedestrians could not hear oncoming horses, buggies, wagons, and trains, and the School for the Deaf was not far from the state School for Imbeciles.

The administration regularly reminded students of the dangers, such as in this news item published in the 1880 edition of *The Companion*: "On Jan. 2nd, Mrs. Kroll, a deaf-mute lady of Minnesota, while walking on the track, was struck by a passing train. She was fearfully mangled and after two hours of terrible agony, death put an end to her sufferings. Mrs. Kroll was a German, and left a husband (hearing) and a two-year old child. When will deaf mutes learn to keep off the Rail Road track?"

The names of twenty-one new pupils appeared that fall in the school newspaper, *The Companion*, including those of Esten and two of his train companions, George Corbett and Oscar Gaarder. Officially, he was "Esten T. Hanson" of Sunburg in Kandiyohi County, even though he hailed from Kerkhoven Township in Swift County, the custom of the school being to identify students by their mailing address.

Esten, given the sequential student number of 420, began in the Primary Class, which ran for four years. Primary Class teachers rarely used textbooks and taught words and phrases using actions and pictures and simple arithmetic. Year five and six students began the Intermediate Class, in which teachers introduced textbooks in history, geography, and arithmetic. The Grammar Class prepared years seven and eight students to use "ordinary" textbooks on ancient and modern history, grammar, arithmetic, bookkeeping, physiology, and abridged versions of natural history and philosophy. After completing Grammar Class, theoretically, students could tackle the hearing world. Two years before Esten began, the average sign class had eighteen pupils and the lip-reading and speech class had forty-six. Unique for its day, the School for the Deaf allowed students a trial period to learn both sign and lip-reading, but if not well suited for the latter, the student continued on only with sign language.

One of Esten's first teachers was Miss Mary Graham, a semi-mute, who had become deaf at age six from meningitis. In 1875, she enrolled as a student and, after training as a seamstress and graduating from the school in 1884, taught there from 1886 to 1888. In November 1887, the Teacher's Association published an article describing her teaching methods in *The Companion*. In essence, this represented Esten's first-year educational experience.

Graham wrote the following about her educational techniques:

> The first day of school is perhaps the hardest of all the others through the whole term, because so many are homesick, and crying to go home, and usually it is difficult to draw their attention to anything. However, I try hard to

interest them by showing them pictures of objects with which they are perfectly familiar such as the cat, horse and dog. I try to encourage them to tell me in their 'home-signs' what they know about them, if they have any at home, etc., and I find this generally interests them very much, and makes them eager to tell me all they can. It often puzzles the teacher to understand the signs they make at first and to talk with them so that they can understand.

When they become familiar with their new home surroundings, the school-room, their teacher, and know that they have come to stay, which is usually in a few days, I commence work in earnest. I begin with the names of common objects familiar to the children. I write a name upon the board, 'dog,' for example, show them a picture of it, talk to them about it, give the sign and teach them how to spell the word. I then tell them to copy the written name on their slates and have them write underneath in columns, then teach them to spell it and remember the sign. This creates an interest and they are eager to learn more names. I continue in this way for a few weeks making a change now and then in the work so that they will not grow weary. A teacher who tries to make the time pass pleasantly and prof-itably to his or her pupils, who is ever on the lookout for some pleasant change when the pupils get tired, is the one who succeeds the best.

After a while I begin on verbs, which I teach by actions, intransitive at first and when they begin to see the meaning clearly I take up transitive verbs. I begin with the present tense and confine my work to that during the entire year. I am careful when teaching the articles 'a' and 'the' and take special pains to make them see the different way in which the two are used, and why. Beginning with arithmetic, I teach the numbers from one to ten. All the exercises of the pupils with these I limit to objects, such as small sticks, crayons, kernels of corn, etc. into groups, the division of pieces of paper into 2, 3, 4, or more equal parts and adding to, or taking away from groups of objects will do more toward giving the children a clear idea of the proper use of numbers than anything else.

Action and object teaching, I find, interests new pupils very much. When actions are used, I call upon a girl to run, and write 'A girl runs.' I ask what she runs on, and they tell me, the floor. I add 'on the floor' to the sentence and so on like this in various ways. I let the pupils be the actors, thus giving them practice in using their names and the pronoun 'I.' I give a great deal of practice in writing, and try to have the children get into the habit of writing plainly. Also I teach them to make the letters of the manual alphabet clearly and correctly, and to learn the right use of signs.

The administration attributed the school's long-term educational success to a system centered on continuity. Eleven years later, in 1898, Superintendent Tate, described one teaching method that contributed to the school's system of continuity: "Blank books, comprising several hundreds of pages, are issued to the teachers of beginning classes, and to start the scheme to all teachers. A summary of all work done is supposed to be copied in these books. The book goes with the class and is a guide to the succeeding teacher. In the end it is a complete history of the class during its entire period in school."

A school day began before 8:00 a.m. with a brief chapel service and then continued until 4:30 p.m., Monday through Friday, with an hour for lunch. In addition to Miss Graham's template, the School for the Deaf taught manners and involved the students in daily calisthenics. The superintendent had concerns for spiritual welfare, too. In the Tenth Biennial Report that was submitted to the governor of Minnesota, the school superintendent described the school's ongoing spiritual efforts: "A brief chapel service in signs is held every morning except Saturday. In addition, on Sunday, classes spend a few minutes in their classrooms. On Sunday afternoon, a brief lecture is delivered upon Bible history. Pupils of advanced classes are expected to reproduce these lectures in tablets and present to the teachers for correction. All moral instruction is of a wholly unsectarian nature. Pupils are allowed to attend churches of the town, when parents wish them to do so."

Esten's routine included writing mandatory monthly letters home. When he wasn't yet able or skilled enough to write in his first year, another student or a teacher wrote for him.

On Saturdays, regular student trips to downtown Faribault brought delight. An 1888 artist's rendition of the city included fifty-nine buildings: churches, schools, businesses, and industry. Faribault hosted ethnic celebrations including St. Patrick's Day and Syttende Mai, the latter of special interest to Esten, whose family always celebrated the Norwegian holiday with music and dance. During Esten's first year, the students celebrated Christmas dinner and greeted Santa Claus, who brought the children gifts. The next evening, teachers entertained students.

As for Esten's trade, his mother, Betsy Hanson, left that choice up to Superintendent Noyes and Esten, who could have studied coopering, shoe-making, tailoring, printing, plain sewing, or dress making. They ultimately decided for Esten to be trained as a printer. Although the campus had the resources and knowledge to teach agriculture, the school's leaders discovered that most boys lacked the interest, probably because of having learned enough at home.

Weekday evenings and Saturday afternoons—after working on a trade in the morning—meant free time for the students, and most of them, girls included, engaged in outdoor activities.

In 1887, Esten's athletic skills were underdeveloped, in part due to an almost complete lack of exposure to organized sports back home. The School for the Deaf was another matter. It was steeped in sports tradition, and to a boy unacquainted with sports, and yet having some athletic ability and an abundance of energy, the School for the Deaf must have seemed a paradise.

The Companion had regular articles about student outdoor activities and sports. The editor mentioned in 1877 that baseball was, "beginning to come in," and noted that the school nurse treated baseball injuries. In 1879, this notice appeared: "On Wednesday afternoon the 'Red Caps' of our Institution had a game with a nine at Shattuck School. At the end of the fourth inning the score was 14 to 10 in favor of our boys, but when the game was stopped by the storm at the end of the sixth inning the Shattuck Club was ahead, 24 to 16."

In the 1880s, *The Companion* mentioned other sports, such as boxing, croquet, running, indoor ten-pin bowling, sledding, lawn tennis, roller skating, bicycling and bicycle racing, skiing, snow-shoeing, ice skating, football, lassoing (taught by a pupil from Montana), and handball. Chess was fashionable in 1887. The gymnasium had dumbbells, Indian Clubs, parallel and horizontal bars, a rowing machine, pulley weights, a striking bag, ladders, climbing ropes, and "Spalding's Health Pulls."

One fad involved boys and girls roller skating in the third-story playroom, which was popular from 1884 into the early '90s. The city of Faribault opened a roller skating rink in 1884. Eighteen pupils had roller skates, and dozens more had them the next school year. Wrote *The Companion*, "The roller-skate [rage] shows no abatement. The treacherous, noisy things were introduced over twenty years ago, and found few buyers." And later, "Roller skating is all the rage now. Lots of the pupils make the house ring with lovely music every day."

On the prairie, Esten could only have dreamed of such well-stocked playgrounds.

CHAPTER FIVE

BASEBALL FEVER

In 1887, organized baseball hadn't yet reached the prairie hinterland of Kerkhoven. Besides, money had been tight at home and Esten would not have had the luxury of being able to purchase a baseball glove, baseball, or a bat. But Esten's arrival at the School for the Deaf coincided exactly with baseball interest blossoming among the student body. By that time, baseball was well established in New York, Boston, and Minneapolis, and had just begun drifting to rural areas of the Midwest; newspaper publishers helped to popularize the sport through their reporting.

As baseball began catching on in Faribault, primarily due to several students bringing it in from Minneapolis, the school newspaper *The Companion* faithfully recorded the game's growth in popularity. Through the lens of *The Companion*, a historian can discern a number of Esten's influences.

While not part of any organized teams early on at school, Esten must have observed, mimicked, and dreamed of playing ball with his more polished classmates, not unlike modern boys who fantasize about playing alongside the pro athletes.

In terms of equipment, the School for the Deaf was a financial have-not among many local "haves," prominent among them ivy-clad Shattuck Academy. Just one example of many: Shattuck had a football field and a number of regulation footballs. The deaf school did not. One reason the school lacked regulation equipment was, in part, because Superintendant Noyes felt uncomfortable requesting additional money for it from the legislature. He ran a responsible, tight ship. As a result, alumni, parents, and outside benefactors ended up donating most of the school's sports equipment, while older students in the trade divisions manufactured uniforms.

The next spring, March 1888, the deaf students caught full-blown baseball fever. *The Companion* described the scene as, "One morning before school last week, our boys played a game of baseball on the snow crust. The score was 9 to 0. We claim that it was the first game of the season."

Enthusiasm for baseball bubbled over. A baseball club consisting of twenty-five boys organized in early April, a time of year in Minnesota that historically has been just at the tail end of a long winter. On May 4, a wave of flurries fell, and a week later so did maddening torrents of rain. The muck led to the canceling of games against Shattuck, which meant not much in the way of baseball transpired that first year before Esten had to return home in early June in time to help with summer farming chores.

The next year wasn't any better. The 1889 season almost was able to start during a thaw in early January, and then, when balmy temperatures continued, the boys actually played a game among themselves at the end of the month. By early March, the older boys were chomping at the bit, and a week later they organized a baseball club, with the first unofficial game happening three weeks later against an off-campus team.

Jay Howard, club secretary, submitted a report for *The Companion*: "The Second nine has played three games of baseball with the Third nine from Shattuck. The nines are very evenly matched, the first game being a tie 8 to 8, the second the Shattucks won 10 to 8, and the third our boys won 6 to 4.... Patrick O'Connor carried off the honors of the first game for our club. His fielding was perfect and in the last inning he made an unassisted double play."

After another victorious contest against Shattuck, the schools butted heads again on May 15, with the School for the Deaf second team defeating the Shattuck second team.

In the late autumn of Esten's third year, in 1889, the older boys crammed in a pick-up game before the onset of winter, and soon thereafter teacher and *The Companion* Editor James Smith campaigned for a better ball field to attract off-campus teams and to improve player safety. Specifically, he wanted a troublesome oak removed from center field. His pen must have carried weight because in mid-April 1890, Superintendant Noyes ordered the tree chopped down, after which, excited about a field finally void of natural obstacles, team members raised money to buy baseball equipment. The baseball fervor and quality of play may have frightened the Shattuck first team. The School for the Deaf played only four games that spring. The Bluffs, the school's first team, split a doubleheader against Morristown; and the Bluff Jrs. lost to a Faribault pick-up team before overwhelming the Shattuck second team, 14-2.

The club secretary reported in *The Companion:* "Wednesday afternoon, May 28, our second nine played another game of baseball, this time with a nine from Shattuck. Before the game began, the opinion that we would get beaten was expressed. The Shattucks scored only two runs and they were gained by two errors, one by Boss, the 2nd baseman, and a wild throw by O'Leary. Those were the only errors made by our club during the game. All the players seemed to be in good trim, especially Bowen, who pitched a great deal better than he did during the previous game. He struck out 7 men in all, while Moon, the pitcher for Shattuck, served 3 in the same way."

The boys had baseball fever, and that would have included religiously following any and all newspaper reports from the Northwestern League concerning the super-hot rivalry between sharp-hitting Minneapolis and St. Paul.

Esten must have waited impatiently for his scrawny frame to mature, so he could begin having his day in the sun. On the train ride home that year, he could have been trying to reconcile his growing excitement about Faribault baseball with the growing tension at home. The Hansons had seen better days financially. Superintendant Noyes had already sent off a number of letters to Tosten, asking for funds to buy Esten clothing, including one letter in early March. Filed with Superintendant Noyes' Minnesota Historical Society collection, the letter reads, "Esten is badly in need of a new suit of clothes, but has no money with which to pay for them. Shall I order a suit for Esten, and if so, will you please send a little money to apply on his account?" A follow-up letter on

May 21 confirmed Esten was wearing a new suit, but the $6 requested to pay for it had not been received.

The unusual hustle and bustle of Kerkhoven, where his father often traded, surprised Esten that year. By 1890, Kerkhoven had become a railroad town of 400, with several times that number living within ten miles. An August 1890 edition of *The Swift County Standard* reported the town as having a roller mill, three grain mills, a town hall, two new churches, a large new school, five general stores, two hardware stores, a drug store, three farm implement dealers, two lumber yards, a jeweler and watchmaker, a physician, one bank, an attorney, a furniture dealer, a land agency and foreign exchange, three hotels, two saloons, three blacksmiths, two shoemakers, a carpenter shop, a barber, a meat market, a livery, and a newspaper.

The Standard brought baseball news to Kerkhoven. A mid-August edition reported that the Appleton baseball team had challenged Benson to a $100 purse, and won, 11-4. A week later, *The Standard* wrote: "A baseball nine composed of small boys came down from Benson last Saturday to play a game of baseball with the Kerkhoven kids. Our boys weren't aware of their coming, so their nine was not all here, and the result was a score of 25 to 29 in favor of Benson. The Kerkhoven kids are bent on trying another game with the Benson third nine. Our boys were not aware that the Bensonites were coming Saturday, and several of the nines were away, others had to take their places, and the boys believe they can beat the Benson boys yet. So another game will come off in the near future."

CHAPTER SIX

THE COMET

While readying for his return trip to school in September 1890, Esten may have learned of a branch of the national Women's Christian Temperance Union (WCTU) organizing in Kerkhoven. This group's mission was to make voters aware of the negative aspects of alcohol and narcotics, with the goal of outlawing them. The WCTU held that a correlation existed between alcohol usage and domestic violence. It lobbied state legislatures to require the teaching of anti-alcohol curricula, with the idea that today's students become tomorrow's voters. (The strategy would pay off in 1918 with passage of the Eighteenth Amendment that prohibited liquor sales and consumption.) The first WCTU meeting in Kerkhoven resulted in eighteen members who signed the pledge: "I hereby solemnly promise, God helping me, to abstain from all distilled, fermented and malt liquors, as a beverage, including wine, beer and cider, and to employ all proper means to discourage the use of and traffic in the same."

The Kerkhoven WCTU immediately flexed its political muscle by petitioning the town council to enact an ordinance prohibiting baseball playing inside town limits on the Sabbath. Many ball players may have drank alcohol, and an initiative to ban Sunday games seemed an easy first step to gain an early victory. The Kerkhoven WCTU had an incremental strategy: do a little here, a little there, winning small victories along the way. However, the town council did not ban the Sunday games.

The first organized baseball game in Kerkhoven history happened on Sunday, September 14, 1890, after twelve-year-old Esten had left for school, when Dublin downed Kerkhoven 22-10 in eight innings, in part due to two of Kerkhoven's best players being absent, and the ailing condition of pitcher Charles Cox.

In Faribault, Esten was learning far more than baseball. Miss Mary Graham would name him as a weekly Roll of Honor student thirteen times. Scholastically, he earned average grades, and, as for character, a 9.0 on a 10-point scale.

His next teacher, Dwight Bangs, who later became superintendent of the North Dakota School for the Deaf, must have had a positive influence on Esten. His scholarship grade skyrocketed to 8.6. At the end of the year, Bangs recommended that Esten be allowed to skip a class the following September, to leapfrog over Eighth to Seventh. The teacher of the Seventh Class, instructor Louis Tuck, a semi-mute, also served as school librarian, and would end up teaching fifty-two years. A tough grader, Tuck named

Esten to the weekly Roll of Honor only twice out of twenty-four possible weeks. In Sixth Class, Mrs. Alice Noyes Smith, also a lip-reading instructor, graded Esten at a solid 8.1 for scholarship. By all objective standards and accounts, by his fourth year, Esten had become an above-average student showing academic promise.

If the idea of playing football was forming in Esten's mind, he must have been greatly disappointed in the fall of 1890 when the older boys pitched in with their spare change to order a new football from Chicago—and then, only a few days after its arrival, had it stolen from an outside windowsill. Undeterred, the boys collected even more money and purchased another football. For the first time, the game really took hold. The boys actually learned the rules—rather than just knocking heads and drawing blood—and significantly improved their playing ability. And right when excitement over football reached a high point, Superintendant Noyes angered an entire campus of male egos by suggesting that football should come to an end because of the violence. His words became prophetic a week later, when John McNeill's collarbone snapped after a vicious tackle. That injury, and others, prompted Noyes to pull the plug on that year's football. In the weeks following, *The Companion* published an article asserting that football was more a sport for beer drinkers and tobacco addicts. And so, with the football season punctured by Noyes, the football-crazy boys had no other alternative than to follow Shattuck, and the University of Minnesota, which defeated Wisconsin 64-0.

As the winter of 1891 gnawed on Esten and other baseball players, compounded by the dullness of chess, checkers, and jack stones, March couldn't arrive fast enough. The players tossed ball late in March, and in the process tossed around smart talk of pushing their passions to the next competitive level, which invariably led to the organization of several school teams. *The Companion* described the scene:

The Star baseball Club met last Monday afternoon in the study room of the boys of the higher classes. The main object was to choose the nines. After roll call, twenty new members were allowed to join the club. William H. Jay, who had been discharged from the club, was allowed to rejoin on condition that he would obey the laws better in the future. Mr. Sampson, the manager, arose and told of Mr. Layton's generosity towards the club. Last term the club became indebted to Mr. Layton for twelve dollars. Two dollars of this amount had since been paid. A short time ago, Mr. Layton informed the manager that he relieved us from paying the rest. An unanimous vote of thanks was tendered him by the club. Mr. Sampson said that the first nine would be more fully uniformed than in the past. Baseball pants have already been ordered and stockings bought. He said he would get some shirts as soon as it could be decided by the Board of Directors. The Treasurer, Mr. Stedman, then gave his report. He stated that the amount now on hand was $2.50 and more would be needed to purchase balls, etc. A motion was made and passed that if necessary we should get players from the city to help us. Mr. Sampson then said that there would be four nines this year.

A boy seldom aspires to greatness without first grasping onto a comet's tail, and the muscular pitching arm of hurler Ed Sampson may have been Esten's comet.

As the sole source of information about baseball during Esten's formative years, *The Companion* prominently mentioned the sporting exploits of only three student-athletes up through 1893: third baseman James O'Leary, second baseman Patrick O'Connor, and pitcher Ed Sampson. O'Leary studied in Faribault from 1880 to 1890 and was seven years older than Esten; O'Connor attended the school from 1884 to 1895 and was three years older; while Ed Sampson had nine years on Esten, and attended from 1882 to 1892, graduating at age twenty-three. All three would fuel Esten's dreams to some degree, including O'Leary years down the road; yet only Sampson could have been the primary agent at this time.

According to all accounts, Ed Sampson was the deaf team's prominent pitcher and influence during Esten's first seven years. In an 1889 game, for example, Sampson hurled the first team to victory, striking out ten while allowing only five hits and four runs. Two years later, the players elected him as their manager. The veteran oiled the boys into peak condition, even joining them in conditioning runs of up to two miles before breakfast, and once, in a ten-mile run. The first team acquired new leather gloves in 1891, and adopted a team motto, "United We Stand, Divided We Fall."

The School for the Deaf prevailed in the opener before losing a nail-biter to Seabury Divinity School, 18-16. The second team conquered its arch rival Shattuck, 10-9, in a rain-shortened affair, in which Shattuck scored all of its nine runs in the first two innings. As in all other years, the 1891 season seemed to end before it began. The school played competitive games on May 11–12, and then rain washed out a scheduled May 23 contest.

While probably playing on the school's fourth team, thirteen-year-old Esten also watched the school's other teams play, and cheered each run—not by shouting, but by signing to peers. The abbreviated baseball season frustrated him.

Spring and summer 1891 brought an explosion of baseball interest on the western Minnesota prairie. In April, *The Swift County Standard* published a letter from Benson saying its third nine had organized, and that Kerkhoven's "boys" owed Benson a game from the previous fall. On May 1, a reporter from Murdock tried waking its boys out of a deep sleep to organize, and the Benson paper reported its nine clearing a diamond and repairing a backstop. Excitement grew over the upcoming Appleton tournament, which Benson won 6-5, with the winning run crossing the plate in the ninth with two outs.

Not to be outdone by his Benson counterpart, the Kerkhoven editor covered his city's July 4 celebration, which began with a cannon blast that roused citizens in early morning just as farm families began arriving. The village band was the highlight of a parade that included a group of eight boys in baseball uniforms carrying a banner describing themselves as "Our Future Heroes." As for the baseball game itself, wrote Editor H. W. Roll of *The Swift County Standard*, "The ball game between the Dublin and Woods [Chippewa County] nines resulted in a victory for the former by a score of 10 to 16. The fireworks in the evening were excellent, and the attendance at the dance fair. We should estimate the attendance during the day at about 2,500 people."

The baseball fever sweeping the prairie finally reached

Kerkhoven later in July, when the newspaper recorded that a "nine comprised of old men of the town" lost to the "Regulars" 22-5. That month, Swift Falls outlasted Murdock, 38-37, and lost to Gilchrist, 27-26, and Benson played Granite Falls and Appleton. Esten could have watched several of these games and oh, what a thrilling time to be an American boy enthralled with baseball!

Yet amid the heavenly stirring, Esten and his family had earthly challenges. *The Swift County Standard* broadcast to the entire county that the Hanson family was in arrears, specifically that proud Tosten owed Swift County $25 in delinquent taxes and accrued penalties.

It became obvious in late 1891 that Superintendant Noyes detested football, yet he mysteriously permitted the ruckus to continue, perhaps because banishing the game outright could have led to a student revolt. The game had become too popular to be quashed at this juncture. That autumn, the older boys purchased a regulation football, and on Halloween word spread around campus, that top athlete and baseball pitcher Ed Sampson had broken his collarbone while playing. That officially gave Noyes the excuse he needed, and in 1891, football was over.

Perpetually worried about student health and safety, Noyes had his hands full in February and March, when a contagious illness spread among students and faculty. To control the outbreak, the administration offered onions, a natural antibiotic. Then Noyes had to deal with baseball. Though not as violent as football, the sport did result in injuries. In March, for instance, Albert Ekberg batted a foul ball that Amiel Henry tried catching with his eye, wrote *The Companion*. "He failed, of course, but his eye was beautifully blackened."

On the prairie in Kerkhoven in 1892, the WCTU was trying to blacken the eye of demon alcohol—one of the few violent acts Superintendant Noyes would ever have supported. The issue reached a boiling point due to pressure dutifully supplied by the WCTU, and so the town fathers scheduled a March election to decide on the issue of making Kerkhoven a "dry" town. In the months before, people outside town limits, angry at the proposed measure, sponsored a number of "wet" parties, which had the effect of taunting the WCTU. Tensions erupted between a pro-liquor shop and saloon owners group and the dry citizens. In a *The Swift County Standard* editorial, "G. Stene" expressed his condemnation of alcohol and addressed the chief objection of store owners: that they had to have alcohol to lure thirsty farmers in for other shopping.

Editor H. W. Roll, a WCTU member, chose this above-the-fold headline in *The Swift County Standard* for Friday, March 11, 1892: "Kerkhoven Went Dry in Last Tuesday's Election for the First Time in its History." The ordinance passed by seven votes. All saloon licenses expired April 1, and a few weeks after that, *The Swift County Standard* ceased publication and quietly moved to Benson. A critical mass of advertisers and subscribers no longer supported a newspaper that was held under WCTU sway, and as a result, Kerkhoven would not have a newspaper for another five years. Of course, the Kerkhoven ordinance didn't affect the drinking freedom of Kerkhoven Township, thus not affecting the Hanson family. However, Esten had signed a mandatory contract with Noyes to shun alcohol over the summer.

In April 1892, to raise money for better baseball equipment, the boys charged fifteen cents admission for an athletic exhibition, which raised the sum of $21. Manager Ed Sampson won the baseball throw event. But all the money raised seemed frozen in time when Mother Nature dumped four inches of snow on the bluff in mid-April. In what may have been an attempt to raise flagging spirits amid the winter rancor, Editor James Smith wrote that week of a recent graduate, James O'Leary, who had been offered $35 to play first base for a hearing team in Anoka, Minnesota. Although a future edition explained that O'Leary had nixed the offer, the story must have intrigued Esten, and opened his mind to the idea of playing baseball professionally.

Signing a professional baseball contract was a major accomplishment for anyone, and even more so for a deaf player who would have difficulty communicating with and being accepted among hearing teammates. Specific to a School for the Deaf student, such as Sampson or Esten, were other significant barriers to excelling at baseball, including the lack of decent off-campus opponents, good coaching, and administration financial support. With few exceptions, their opponents were Shattuck and local Faribault teams, which constituted Esten's only opportunities to sharpen his diamond skills. As a student, he no doubt wanted more exposure after reading in the Gallaudet College newspaper of the amazing professional exploits of deaf major leaguer Dummy Hoy. Esten read the newspaper accounts, sensed the competitive juices at games, felt the soft leather of the glove on his hand, ran his fingers up and down the stained ash bat—heck, he could taste the game of baseball—and yet he could never get enough of it at school to satisfy his hunger.

In the 1892 season, after the rain finally ceased and the clouds parted, permitting the sun to shine in all its glory, the temperature warmed up sufficiently for the boys of spring to retake their positions. Minnesota School for the Deaf played just three games that year against off-campus teams: a doubleheader against Seabury Divinity School, and a single game the next day against Shattuck.

Said Editor James Smith on May 7:

The first game of the season came off Friday afternoon between the first nine of Seabury School, and our first nine, on the grounds of the former, and resulted in an over-whelming victory for our club. The weather was very disagreeable, but both nines braced up and began the battle with much enthusiasm. Griffith pitched for the Seabury nine and did some good work. In the first inning our club scored no runs. Sampson, our best pitcher, filled the box for our club, while Squire Stedman was behind the bat. Sampson began by knocking out his men in regular order while Squire Stedman picked the balls from behind the bat with much ease. The umpiring was at first done by one of the Seabury players but Mr. Smith was chosen in his place. Squire Stedman did some excellent batting indeed. He beat both our nine and the Seabury nine at bat. He scored two home runs and two three-base hits. He would have scored one of the three-base hits had he passed the first base without stum-bling and hurting himself. When he arrived at the third base Jay had to take his place. Pat O'Connor our second baseman and George Renkes did some good work both in the field and at bat. The Seabury nine did some good batting. Some two base hits were scored by them and our nine.

Ed Sampson struck out at least ten batters in every game that spring.

On May 31, 1892, a local photographer took a Minnesota School for the Deaf team photo that included Esten Hanson with a catcher's pad on his left hand. He was dressed in knee-high stockings, baseball pants, a white shirt, tied necktie, and a visored cap. An older player had his hands on Esten's shoulders. Reclining in the front row, one player wore a "Stars" uniform, marking that person alone as a first teamer.

The School for the Deaf did not list Esten on the first or second team roster in 1892. The photograph revealed eleven individuals frozen in time, a puzzle to our generation as to who exactly was on the team. The photo could have been the third team, its 1892 captain or Manager Ed Sampson, and a "sub" from the first nine. Esten could have been the third team catcher or regularly subbed for the second team. As Esten's manager, Ed Sampson must have taught him catching and pitching skills, including ways to throw curves and fastballs, the necessities of control and placement, and hand signals calling for certain pitches. The 1892 baseball season afforded Esten one last precious opportunity to practice alongside graduating Ed Sampson.

CHAPTER SEVEN

CHICAGO WORLD'S FAIR

A flood of good sentiment must have swept over Esten after he scanned the Minneapolis News column in the October 20 issue of *The Companion*. In it, he learned that former pitcher Ed Sampson had bagged twenty-three pigeons while hunting in Osseo, Minnesota. Pretty good shooting for a "baseballist," penned the Minneapolis reporter.

Early in November 1892, James Smith, teacher at the School for the Deaf and editor for *The Companion*, lectured students on the history of "Sports and Amusements," describing the amusements of Egyptians, Greeks, and Romans before gradually addressing modern times. He gave accounts of the cruel and barbarous sports of the Roman amphitheater, where thousands of wild beasts and human beings bled and died "to make a Roman holiday." After speaking of the Middle Ages "tournament" and Spanish bullfights, and using blackboard drawings of various sports objects, he lectured on the popular sports of the day, including American baseball, English cricket, Canadian lacrosse, football, lawn tennis, croquet, bowling, chess, and checkers.

At this point in his schooling, Esten had already finished two years of printing training and five years of articulation. Noyes possibly helped Esten choose printing as a trade after watching him excel in the English language his first two years. Printers had to know how to write and spell well, use proper grammar, and lip-read enough to understand hearing coworkers. His baseball career proved Esten had exceptional hand-eye coordination, another essential ingredient. A printing industry training theoretically ensured that Esten would have a livelihood after leaving school.

In his sixth year, he began receiving school recognition for his lip-reading talents, and the timing couldn't have been better: The Chicago World's Fair was scheduled for 1893.

The State of Minnesota constructed a building on the Chicago exhibition grounds to display the Minnesota Educational Exhibit, which would highlight the state's higher education, normal schools, city schools, rural schools, and special schools, such as the Minnesota School for the Deaf. Dr. Noyes chose to exhibit work from Esten's lip-reading class, and, from that class, the work of only six students. In particular, Esten's work arose from an exercise in which his teacher had read the students ten questions and asked them to describe a picture in an instructional book, *The Riverside Language Pictures*. After reading the teacher's lips, Esten wrote down the questions and his answers. Using neatly written answers, Esten correctly described the scene and then under the teacher's direction transferred his work to a standardized form. This exercise would become the only surviving example of his handwriting, lip-reading, writing, and English progress at school. In addition to copying his work verbatim, the teacher noted the work was accomplished by "Esten Hanson in class on March 8, 1893, taking thirty minutes to complete the exercise." Further notes explained that Esten was fifteen, was congenitally deaf, and had been an articulation student for thirty minutes a day for more than five years.

The spring of 1893 would not be the same, and the baseball team not the school's best, as bigger-than-life Ed Sampson, who had dominated school athletics for more than six years, had graduated and was now pitching in Minneapolis. The team tried its best, though. The schedule began in earnest with a shellacking, a 15-0 loss to Shattuck. The school regained a modicum of pride in a 16-15 win over Faribault High, but not much, because in that game, a fly ball hit deaf student Hiram Bailey between the eyes.

Wrote Editor James Smith after another game, "Our boys are not great ball players this year. Our baseball nine went over to Shattuck school last Wednesday afternoon and played a game with the Shattuck second nine. The weather was cold and raw; and the game was full of errors and bad plays on both sides, though our boys made the worst blunders. The result was Shattuck 24, our boys 7. There is a lack of practice and discipline in our nine. Next year we hope it will be different."

That last game must have embarrassed Esten, when the School for the Deaf first team soundly went down to defeat 24-7 against a Shattuck second team. Truly, the deaf team missed Ed Sampson's effective pitching, inner drive for commitment and unity, and managerial talent and knowledge.

Any momentum Dr. Noyes had from preparing for and laboring at the Chicago World's Fair in summer 1893 came to an abrupt halt when he began to experience health problems. The fair had been a once-in-a-lifetime event. Also known as the World's Columbian Exposition, the Chicago World's Fair marked the 400 anniversary of Christopher Columbus's discovery of America, and it drew more than twenty-seven million people, well over the equivalent of a third of the population of the entire United States. The fair contained more than 200 buildings, including Minnesota's, on a huge 600-acre campus. Never before had such a massive fair been held in America, and the naturally nervous Noyes never before had experienced anything vaguely akin to it. The nation, and the world, visited, including Americans Thomas Edison, Andrew Carnegie, J. P. Morgan, Helen Keller, Frederick Douglass, Susan B. Anthony, and President Grover Cleveland. Millions of Americans must have passed right by the school's exhibit.

Noyes had been hired as superintendent in 1866 after fourteen years of experience in deaf education. In many ways, Noyes *was* the Minnesota School for the Deaf, leaving his mark on virtually every aspect of the organization, from its spiritual emphasis, to admissions, academics, food menus, and the individual lives of students. Noyes even wrote notes to parents concerning minor overdue bills.

In *The Minnesota School for the Deaf 1863–1963*, author Wesley Lauritsen wrote, "Dr. Noyes stated it was no easy task to bring all in the school up to the standard of the Golden Rule. He said that to a large extent the government and discipline of the school must depend upon the superintendent. Dr. Noyes got weekly reports from staff members and monitors on the conduct of each and every student and these reports helped the superintendent get a good picture of the behavior of each student in the school."

But his health forced him to take a one-year leave, announced secretary of the board, Rodney Mott, at the start of the 1893 school year. Said Noyes in his Eighth Biennial Report to the state legislature, "The necessity arose in consequence of my illness to which I was inadvertently subjected by reason of an indisposition, caused by overwork incident to the extra labor of the world's congress, together with other unusual work."

The board chose Charles Gillett, of Illinois, as an interim superintendent. To improve baseball team morale, either Gillett or Noyes—if the latter, then a final goodwill gesture—ordered the grounds north of Barron Hall leveled to construct a baseball diamond.

Noyes' health aside, school life went on as usual. Once again, Editor James Smith, in covering baseball, mentioned only the achievements of first and second team players; but he did mention Esten's name twice, as a wild game trapper and a snow-sledding enthusiast. The first mention indirectly linked Esten with second baseman Pat O'Connor, who, along with John Clauson and other boys, walked down Cannon City Road together on a day in December. O'Connor noticed something in front of him, ran fast, and gave the "thing" a swift kick in the air. When the "thing" fell, Clauson immediately cut off its head. When gathering around it, the boys suddenly realized Clauson had decapitated a skunk—at least this was the boys' story. A week later, *The Companion* reported, "O'Connor displayed a totally different and heartfelt attitude towards God's Creatures when he was credited for counseling Esten Hanson that the proper way to dispose of a blue jay caught by Esten in his rabbit trap was to release the bird from captivity."

Perhaps in O'Connor, a future valedictorian, sixteen-year-old Esten had a perfect soul mate. In fact, Esten could have been one of the "other boys" who witnessed the decapitation. Appearing in January, the second news item reported that Esten had spied a black-tailed ermine while sledding down Eighth Street hill.

Along with kinder temperatures came baseball fever again, and Esten began playing ball that year in the first week of March with the second team, on the field next to Barron Hall. The first 1894 intra-squad game happened in mid-March, and after it, the Athletic Association elected Pat O'Connor as secretary, Charles Boss as president, and Hiram Bailey, the player hit between the eyes the previous year, as vice president. On March 31, Smith faithfully described the ingenuity of one player, writing, "Engmar Kvittem wanted a pair of trousers to play baseball and to run in. He got two empty flour sacks. The sacks were white and he did not want his new trousers to be white so he dyed the sacks black in some dye he made himself by soaking butternuts in water. Mr. Beupre (the school's tailoring instructor) told him how to do it. He cut out the trousers and sewed them on the sewing machine in the tailor shop. Now he has a pair of trousers to play in that are the envy of all the other boys."

As for other boys, Smith wrote, "Howard Jay claims he was first to set the fashion among the boys of wearing heel-less shoes. He has had several imitators. George Corbett has a new pair of shoes. He had them made without heels, because he thinks shoes are better without heels. They were a little tight, so George got Henry Appel to wear them a few days to make them large enough to be comfortable on his own feet."

The first game was a nine-inning affair between the Minnesota School for the Deaf first-team "Stars" and the Shattuck first and second teams. Wrote Smith, "At first it seemed as if our boys would be badly beaten; especially at the end of the fifth inning, when the score was II to 4 against us. But in the sixth inning we batted the ball freely, piling up seven runs, and tying the score. From that time on, the game was close and exciting. When the Stars had finished the ninth inning, and before the Shattucks began it, the score was I4 to I3 in favor of the Stars. Two men were put out and the victory seemed ours. Then the Shattucks got two men on bases, and by errors they managed to score, winning the game.... Although our boys failed to win, they have no reason to feel other than satisfied. They put up a good game and showed many signs of improvement over last year's work."

It was sn encouraging effort. The Stars gained a bit of revenge on May 30, by beating the local cadets I6-I5. School ended six days later. Esten, with an empty feeling after another unsatisfying season, would ride the train the very next day from Faribault to Kerkhoven for the seventh time.

As the Great Northern carried him west out of Minneapolis toward Kerkhoven, swaying and lurching over crossings and switches, Esten may have been reminded of his first trip into the unknown from Kerkhoven to Faribault. It seems like only yesterday, he must have thought. By any stretch of the imagination, Esten Hanson was not the same person as he was seven years before. In 1887, at age nine, he had not been able to read lips, and could say out loud only the words "mama" and "papa" and two letters of the alphabet. By 1894, he fluently read lips.

In part due to his attending Sunday school, chapel, and even regular classes, Esten had gained a knowledge of Christian morals, the Bible, salvation, forgiveness, the Trinity, and God. Further, he had learned to respect girls, elders, and persons in authority. For the first time, he had made non-Norwegian friends—even Irish friends named O'Leary and O'Connor, who celebrated St. Patrick's Day. He had learned of other cultures and countries. It was a great big world, far bigger than what he had grown up among in Swift County years earlier.

He had had five years of training as a printer. The deaf school had introduced him to dozens of games, ones non-existent in Kerkhoven, and through playing them he had learned about team-work. He had learned about winter sports, such as skiing, bobsledding, and coasting down Eighth Street hill. He had learned to ice skate on the Straight River. Noyes had reminded him to keep a healthy body, mind, and spirit, and to shun liquor and tobacco.

Esten could play baseball and had learned the game from the best: Sampson and O'Connor. He had held a steady 8.0 average for scholarship, learning the gamut from language, arithmetic, and penmanship, to calisthenics, manners, and morals.

Best of all, he had learned he was no different in spirit than any hearing child, nor was he a freak or a circus sideshow feature— he just couldn't hear. All considered, he could survive well in the hearing world, in part because young men such as Ed Sampson had led the way.

Esten had come a long way in these years at Faribault. As the train approached Kerkhoven depot, Esten guessed that his father and three brothers would be waiting for him. He waved goodbye to

George Corbett and Ernest Gerard, and from there, after a brief reunion—Norwegian men were reluctant to show their emotions, especially in public—the Hanson men rode the prairie together eleven miles to Monson Lake. Esten used what sign language his brothers could understand. Presumably, the summer would be another one filled with chores, field work, and some fishing, and if lucky enough, he would play a little baseball. Already, he was mulling over his fall return to school in Faribault, and playing another season of baseball, and then he perhaps realized, for the first time, that he might be able to make the first team.

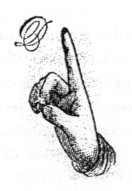

CHAPTER EIGHT

GREAT PANIC

A photograph taken in mid-June 1894, appearing years later in the November 8, 1944, *Willmar Weekly Tribune*, showed sixteen-year-old Esten Hanson and his older brother, Hans, as members of the Sunburg baseball team. The picture had been taken eleven days after the close of the 1893–94 school year and twelve days after the school's first team had beaten Shattuck. The occasion of the picture was a picnic near the West Norway Lake Church, four miles southeast of the Hanson farm. The picture captured Esten as relatively short compared to other players, yet with a muscular build. His body language suggests that he was comfortable and felt he belonged, looking directly into the camera lens. Baseball made for an enjoyable summer, a welcome respite from the labors of their daily farming routine.

In September, only six days prior to the start of school, Tosten wrote returning Superintendant Noyes, who was now back from his year of rest, to ask if the board had indeed approved Esten for three additional years beyond the basic seven-year course. His question seemed logical because not all students earned the extension. The support shown by Noyes, below, should have erased any doubt in Tosten's mind of Esten's potential.

September 8, 1894
Tosten Hanson, Sunburgh [sic], Minn.
Dear Sir:
Replying to yours of the 6th would say that Esten has been granted three years additional time in school by our Board of Directors, and it is very desirable that he attend regularly until he quits school for good. A pupil loses very much in staying out a year. If Esten wishes to attend school here anymore he should return this year. Our school will be very full this year, and he should return as soon as possible. Hoping to see him next week, I am
Yours Very Truly,
J. L. Noyes, Supt.

The Hansons made the difficult decision to keep Esten home. Tosten and Betsy likely discussed at least three possibilities: Esten's permanently leaving school to help on the farm, Esten's leaving for only a year to temporarily suspend Tosten's financial obligation, and Esten's returning on time or late to school. Assuming Esten desired to return, a number of external factors could have influenced their decision. Foremost, a huge number of American workers had fallen upon hard times following The Great Panic of

1893, the worst economic crisis in American history to that point, which resulted in more than 15,000 companies, 500 banks, and three major railroads going out of business, including the Union Pacific. In July 1894, Pullman workers went on strike, effectively shutting down the nation's passenger railroad system. The situation in 1894 became so acute that Tosten could have determined he had to have Esten on the farm, and couldn't afford sending any money to Noyes for his care. (*The Companion* reported that Noyes was surprised when the economic panic did not significantly decrease enrollment that fall, and also: "We are all sorry that the hard times have thrown so many of our deaf friends in Minneapolis and St. Paul out of work.")

Not wealthy by any definition, the Hansons indirectly relied on the railroad system to transport their wheat to Minneapolis, and with the recent collapse of several railroads, Tosten could have weighed his options carefully. Esten, with an iron back and muscular arms, could help on the farm. Tosten's decision—if it was his primarily—also could have been influenced by Esten's obvious advancements in lip-reading, English, and sign language. Esten may have been educated enough, in his eyes. If not returning to school had been Esten's choice, perhaps Esten may have been tired of the classroom, and of his printing training, of which his five years of experience were enough to find decent employment. Or maybe Esten was aware of his father's difficulties and did not want to create more problems. This could help spare the family from further embarrassment. Finally, due to his father's regularly failing to send money to Noyes, Esten may have become weary—and embarrassed—of having to wear much-used clothing, and of Noyes having to beg his father for funds.

Why return in September 1895? For one, the economic fallout

that year may have been significantly less than Tosten had anticipated. Esten may have missed school and friends—he probably was
receiving the school newspaper—or he could have been in love with
a Faribault girl, or realized his likelihood of finding a mate was
vastly improved there. Another possibility: Betsy could have
persuaded both her husband and son of the importance of
continuing his education.

While reading the school newspaper during his missed 1894–95
school year, at times, Esten must have been very anxious to return.
In March, baseball became the burning topic among the school-
boys, with some fashioning their own leather gloves and others
collecting funds to purchase equipment from Spaulding. *The
Companion* published a bevy of baseball news in April: "The boys
seem to be playing pretty good ball. The fourth nine of our boys
played a game of ball with a nine of town boys last Saturday afternoon, and won by a score of 18 to 11."

Dr. Noyes steadfastly refused the boys' request to cut down the
ball field apple tree, which seemed out of character for someone
habitually worried about student health and safety. Within weeks
after his apple tree decision, Noyes, who had discharged his duties
for about thirty years, officially submitted his permanent resignation, his anesthetized letter giving the board a generous fifteen
months' notice. This was not announced publicly; the news didn't
reach the pages of *The Companion*. Out in rural Swift County, Esten
certainly would not have known of Noyes' resignation, but through
The Companion, he did keep track of Patrick O'Connor being named
class valedictorian, Jacob Rebenovitz being badly hurt by a batted

ball, and Engmar Kvittem securing a black eye from a Mike Roizowiez foul. On May 18, the Shattuck nine beat the School for the Deaf first team, 21-10. A week later, a newspaper article of a Sunday school concert included the name of Esten's good friend, Anthony Lykken.

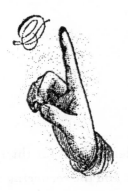

CHAPTER NINE

TRIUMPHANT RETURN

No one knows why Esten returned for the 1895–96 school year. An August 22 letter from the departing superintendent, Dr. Noyes, cited a correspondence of two days before.

> Tosten Hanson
>
> Sunburgh [sic], Minn.
>
> Dear Sir:
>
> Replying to yours of the 20th. In regard to Esten's returning to school would say that he will be received providing he reports promptly Wednesday Sept. 11th. The state provides this school, free, and it is not right to keep a pupil out even a few weeks. Remember, if Esten comes back to school he must come when the term commences. Also

remember to send a deposit of five or ten dollars to apply on his clothing account.

Very Respectfully,

J. L. Noyes, Supt.

Managing a 200-student school for thirty years had taken its toll on Jonathan L. Noyes, and the recurring correspondence with Esten's father was not appreciated. As for Esten, upon returning, he felt the excitement of catching up with old school friends. Nearly eighteen, he had a taste for baseball, and was acquiring a thirst for what the game could offer him—clean fun, pride of accomplishment, and the potential for earning money. It had become the national pastime, and Esten was permanently hooked, first by Sampson, and then by O'Leary and O'Connor.

Entering Faribault for his final three years, eighteen-year-old Esten Hanson would need financial assistance of some sort, and plenty of encouragement. His father had been lax sending money, and it took exactly one day for the new superintendent, James Tate, to once again have to remind Tosten of his financial obligations. His letter also mentioned that Esten wished to transfer to the cabinet shop, and that, "Boys are not allowed to change their trade without some good reason." Esten's reasons for requesting a transfer evidently were not sufficient in the eyes of Superintendent Tate, as Esten continued learning the printing trade during his final three years of school.

In November, *The Companion* called Esten an "outdoorsman," who "lost rabbit number two the other day. He had it in a trap but it wriggled out and ran away. He forgot to put salt on its tail." The article mentioned Fred Von Rueden, Jo Kucera, and Esten as forming a partnership to catch rabbits, and the article ended with, "The long eared, bobtailed inhabitants of the woods are hereby warned that if they hope to see the posies bloom in the spring, they had better emigrate, or crawl into their burrows and pull the holes in after them."

The Companion reported days after Christmas, "Esten Hanson's sister spent Christmas here with him." It wasn't uncommon for family members to visit campus on holidays, but this was the first and only recorded instance of a Hanson family member visiting Esten, and two weeks later, she was still there. Caroline, his older sister, was hired as an employee, at $12 per month, beginning on February 1, as shown in school records. This might have been an ideal solution. Caroline understood some sign language, needed to earn a paycheck, and with a full-time job she could help support Esten's schooling, as well as keep tabs on the young man. After this, Superintendant Tate—unlike prior years when Noyes had to plead with Tosten continually—only twice had to write financial pleas to Tosten over Esten's final three years.

A baseball club formed early in February 1896. The weather in late January and early February was unseasonably warm and dry enough for play, allowing the first nine to beat the second, 9-7. As the weather returned to seasonal norms, the younger boys, distraught because the older boys had all the baseballs, began unraveling their mittens and stockings to wind the yarn into baseballs. The older boys played the last day of February, and, to get physically fit, began exercising in the gym. Perhaps remembering the strict training regimen of Ed Sampson, Manager Fred Anderson ordered the boys to take long runs before breakfast, perhaps to give the School for the Deaf team a conditioning edge over Shattuck. By late March, the boys were practicing almost daily, which in southern Minnesota certainly would have included temperatures in the 30s and 40s. Even the girls made plans to play, prompting Editor James Smith to comment in a chauvinistic manner: "Is this a result of leap year or of the 'new woman' movement?"

Included in Anderson's responsibilities was the difficult and unenviable task of selecting the first and second nines, the Stars, and the Stars Jrs. The official Stars line-up picked by Anderson was as follows: Charles Grady, catcher; Esten Hanson, pitcher; Fred Anderson, first base; Sarom Olson, second base; Arlo Watson, third base; George Corbett, shortstop; Michael Frank, center field; Frederick Von Rueden, right field; and Edward Montcalm, left field.

Grady hailed from Hennepin County, and was a relative newcomer, having been admitted in 1894. Twenty-year-old Manager Fred Anderson came from Anoka County, was born congenitally deaf, and had a deaf brother and sister. He was in the printing trade, like Esten.

Twenty-three-year-old Sarom Olson, of Swedish heritage, from Goodhue County, became deaf from brain fever at age two, and was learning printing.

Arlo Watson was seventeen, and from Wabasha County. A Canadian Scot, he and a sister were born deaf. Like Olson, Anderson, and Esten, he was training to be a printer.

Nineteen-year-old George Corbett of Clay County, Esten's

long-time train companion, was born deaf to Irish parents and wanted to be a cooper.

Studying to be a shoemaker was twenty-seven-year-old Michael Frank of Nicollet County. Having a German heritage, he became deaf after an earache at age six months and had a deaf great-aunt and great-uncle.

Frederick Von Rueden became deaf at age two from sunstroke. The nineteen-year-old Faribault native had a deaf brother and German parents.

Rounding out the nine was a Polk County native, nineteen-year-old Edward Montcalm, of French-Canadian heritage, who had become deaf at ten months due to brain fever, and also had a deaf aunt.

The Hanson family, including Esten's brothers and sisters, closely followed the school newspaper for information related to Esten's baseball exploits. Caroline attended some of the games and wrote home of her impressions. In his required monthly letter home, Esten no doubt told of having been chosen for the prestigious first team.

Commenting on the March weather (on April 4, 1896), *The Companion* said: "March went out like a raging lion, roaming, with eyes flashing, mane waving and tail swishing." It rained buckets. With April came snow and more snow, and in the muck, the first and second nines slushed to a 7-7 tie, and then came another eight inches of snow, and then, just as suddenly, a dry southern wind. The snow melted, the field dried, and the Stars played Faribault High while the girls watched the baseball game from the second

floor piazza of the main building. The Stars broke to a 13-1 lead
after two innings to beat the locals 18-9, and Esten had only one
bad stretch, yielding four runs in the fifth. It was his first official
outing on the first team, and it had to feel great. Three days later,
he grabbed another winning decision against Faribault High, this
time hitting second in the line-up and pitching his team to an 8-5
triumph in a snappy ninety minutes over five innings, having done
"very brilliant work," wrote Editor James Smith.

His streak ended in late April, when he dropped a 10-3 decision to a Shattuck hurler. Caroline encouraged him to do better in
the next game. Esten had carried the hopes and expectations of
200 deaf students on his broad shoulders. *The Companion* reported
on the loss, almost apologetically, saying, "Esten Hanson is our
best pitcher. His arm is not yet in good condition to pitch a full
game. When he gets toughened he will do better, it is hoped.
Edward Montcalm is his substitute. Ed has a swift delivery, but is
not up in curves."

Temperatures in Faribault skyrocketed to 80 degrees around
May 1, and Esten's confidence rose with it—outside of baseball.
Days after his last game, he appeared in a Sunday school program
that opened with a welcome and The Lord's Prayer, and continued
with students giving biblical presentations in sign language,
covering such topics as the Ten Commandments, selected Psalms
readings, hymns, and the Beatitudes. Fred Anderson spoke on,
"Let not your heart be troubled," and Esten Hanson, with William
Peters, presented the Beatitudes in responsive reading. This
Sunday school event marked the only known instance of Esten

Hanson ever making a presentation in front of the student body and faculty. Apparently, at age eighteen, Esten was now capable and comfortable signing before an audience. His self-confidence was growing by leaps and bounds.

The Companion described the April 24 game: "Last Friday afternoon a Faribault picked nine came upon our grounds for a game. Soon the umpire called play, and the game began. In the commencement of the innings, the picked nine scored more runs than the Stars, but further on the Stars carefully worked hard, and Esten Hanson, our pitcher, did very excellent work, and they scored more runs than the picked nine, and defeated them by a score of 13 to 11. It was a close and exciting game."

Inning:	1	2	3	4	5	6	7	8	9	
FPN:	3	3	4	0	0	0	0	1	0	—11
Stars:	0	2	3	1	1	2	4	0	x	—13

Home run, S. Olson.

Umpire, Kilpatrick.

Scorer, E. Kvittem.

Time of game, 1 1/2 hours.

The next week, the team could think of nothing but *baseball, baseball, baseball,* and the boys boldly handed Superintendant Tate a petition requesting a half-day holiday to take advantage of the fine weather so they could play a baseball game against archrival Shattuck. After Tate agreed, and the students took their holiday, Shattuck mysteriously backed out.

The boys didn't have to wait long to play. On May 4, Esten

pitched his best game to date, this one against the Voodoo Club, an older Faribault team. If Manager Anderson had doubts about Esten's rubbery arm, his worries vanished for good after this effort, because he hurled a nine-inning game, struck out twelve, and completely silenced the opposition after yielding three first-inning runs. The 17-3 count over two hours was a one-sided affair. Not to be outdone, the Voodoo Club, the following week, brought along a number of ringers to down the Stars 8-5 in seven innings. Esten sprained his ankle early in the game and had to yield the mound to substitute Edward Montcalm, who, "pitched very swiftly, though somewhat wild, and struck out five." After his injury, Esten went out to play right field, Montcalm's regular spot. The Voodoo Club abruptly left the field after seven innings to unofficially end the hotly contested game, despite vehement protests from the Stars.

The Stars and Voodoo Club met again. This time, the Stars broke out to a first-inning 4-0 lead, and then Edward Montcalm ambled to the mound in place of Esten and his tender ankle. *The Companion* said, as if trumpeting the necessity of playing Esten, "... but great disappointment appeared to the Stars as a result of the poor pitching of Montcalm, which caused the scoring of 7 runs by the Voodoos. The Stars proved very careless both in batting and fielding and they made many errors. The result was victory for the Voodoos by a score of 11 to 8 points in seven innings. The Stars might have gained the victory if Hanson had pitched for the Stars in the first inning. Hanson took the place of Montcalm in the second inning and did better work, and the Voodoos scored only four runs in the remaining innings. Hanson struck out 8, and Montcalm 1, and the Voodoos, 8. It was a very hot and exciting game."

In the three games for which Minnesota School for the Deaf kept statistics, Esten struck out twenty-one, and walked three, and he obviously was a pitcher in command of his game. He was in superb physical condition, could throw fastballs and curves, and given his tutelage over the years by mentor Ed Sampson, understood the game of pitch and catch as well as anyone. Two weeks later, Esten and teammate George Corbett boarded the early train to Minneapolis and, seated together, reflected on the most exciting baseball season in school history. It was their day to shine, and they grasped at every last ray of glory.

CHAPTER TEN

JUST BASEBALL

Noyes officially left and Tate began as superintendent on June 1, 1896. In his first report to the legislature, Tate praised the retiring of Dr. Noyes, "How much of muscle, of brain, of nervous energy this noble man spent in these thirty years cannot be reckoned by the ordinary rules of computation. Suffice it to say that he left a monument, not only in this pile of splendid buildings, but one more lasting in the hearts of the deaf in Minnesota. We would join them in strewing flowers along the way of Jonathan L. Noyes." Following his financial request of $150,000 for two years of the school's budget, Tate added, "We confidently commit this institution to the keeping of the Providence under the shadow of whose wing she has been thus preserved."

In Tate's report to Governor Clough, certain philosophies and commitments stood out: Tate wasn't satisfied with the status quo, would improve the aging facilities, and would make every effort to expand opportunities for the girls, whom he felt needed more occupational choices.

On September 9, 1896, the first day of the school year, Esten Hanson was nowhere to be found. With Noyes out, Tosten apparently had calculated that he could get away with keeping Esten back a few weeks to help harvest the crops. Esten's sister Caroline, who was ready to work another school year full-time, probably notified Tate in advance of the delay. Esten had experienced—and enjoyed—his first publicly recognized baseball season only six months earlier; teachers loved him; he had above-average grades, and Caroline was already there. He had no other reason to delay. But he did finally show up.

Although baseball was his true love, Esten also liked the running and tackling of raucous campus football, and he rejoiced when he found out that Superintendant Tate tolerated the sport more than Noyes. Tate, a lawn tennis and baseball athlete, allowed the boys to play football no-holds-barred, and they continued in that wild vein until the pigskin permanently deflated over Halloween week. After that, the boys smartly chose up sides and made do with meek baseball, Edward Montcalm pitching.

The winter of 1896–1897 crept along at a snail's pace—or so it seemed to baseball boys fantasizing of hitting home runs, throwing strikeouts, and receiving public acclaim. There wasn't much else to do. Some of the more romantically inclined boys linked up with female friends on the rickety sofa in the main hall second floor, until the sofa broke one night, curtailing that social outlet.

Boy-girl relationships at the school in the 1890s involved such benign activities as hand holding, ice skating, parlor games, and sitting—on opposite sides—of the same dining room table.

Desperate for a stopgap measure, and lucking upon a January thaw, twenty-two of the older boys cleared away enough snow to play football. Their action led that day to at least two players acquiring black eyes: Henry Bruns and Christian Nelson. In early February, a friend of Esten from Swift County, probably Lue Evenson, visited, and temporarily rescued the spirits of Esten and his sister from the winter doldrums.

After the visitor left, Esten's thoughts, for a while, at least, turned fully toward baseball—assuming his mind had ever left it. As usual, the boys elected club officers in early March, including expert batter Charles Grady as manager and first team captain. (Frederick Anderson had graduated in June 1896.) But rather than baseball, most of the boys were caught up that winter in predicting the upcoming March 17 heavyweight boxing title bout in Nevada between Gentleman Jim Corbett and New Zealander Bob Fitzsimmons. The boys were aware of the event—probably too much so as Editor James Smith gently brought them to their senses on March 6, saying: "Some of our boys think and talk a great deal about the fight that is to take place in Nevada, March 17. We think that they could find many better things to think and talk about than that."

Learning that Fitzsimmons put Corbett down for the count in the fourteenth round, and heeding Smith's advice, the boys once more readied themselves for the new season. When tossing around a baseball in early April, and stinging their fingertips from the harsh cold, the boys felt much better after hearing that Superintendant Tate had just purchased regulation baseballs, ash bats, a catcher's mask, and a chest protector. Esten, while not making baseball news on April 10, did attract Editor James Smith who wrote (without elaboration): "Esten Hanson is wearing a pair of gold-bowled spectacles. They give him quite a dignified look until he smiles."

At his first opportunity, probably the next practice, Manager Charles Grady told the team in no uncertain terms, with hands and fingers flying accompanied by negative facial expressions, that their last baseball performance was a total embarrassment—that they played like beginners. The official game description smacked of an across-the-board failure, from lousy throwing, fielding, hitting, and base running, to judgment errors. The final score damaged school pride, and the 10-9 rematch loss didn't help. Editor James Smith tried cheering the boys by saying that when he played in "the good old days," the School for the Deaf lost to Shattuck "something like 75-20."

The School for the Deaf had only two games all spring, and Esten's baseball highlight that year would be witnessing Shattuck beat Mankato High.

At the school picnic in late May, Esten's name wasn't listed as a participant in any of the athletic events, such as the eighty-yard run, sack race, three-legged race, and ball throwing or catching. But his friend George Corbett participated and placed first or second in every scheduled event, which won him prizes, including nuts, candy, popcorn, and writing tablets.

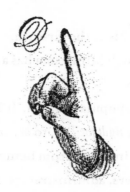

CHAPTER ELEVEN

VAST IMPROVEMENT

Esten was no longer the wide-eyed, bewildered, nine-year-old boy journeying to Faribault to learn how to talk with his hands. By 1897, he certainly had the sequence of railroad stops memorized, and in age, he was only a month shy of twenty. Normally, friend George Corbett and he gabbed summer ball exploits on the way back, but this year, Esten wasn't anywhere to be found on the train—he would show up for school two weeks late.

It would be Esten's last trip to Faribault. Student life was like a vacation when compared to the rigors of farming. At least the Hanson farm was finally prospering, having expanded to more than 300 acres.

When Esten arrived, school was already in progress. He learned, for instance, of a new first-year student while reading the October 9 *Companion*: "Last week a little half-breed Indian girl was admitted to the school. This is the first time that one of her race has been a pupil here, though Minnesota has a considerable Indian population."

Bicycling had become popular as well. It had taken about five years for the song, *A Bicycle Built for Two*, to actually have meaning in Faribault, and no one was immune from being bitten by the bicycle bug—boys and girls, teachers, administrators. Money played a large part in who owned a bicycle, and who didn't; few students had one. Newspapers of the day reported on the tribulations of balancing on and controlling the newfangled contraptions, and on the numerous collisions involving bicycles and street cars, trains, people, dogs, shrubbery—anything. Six teachers that fall rode their bicycles the twenty-four miles to Morristown and back, taking about six hours.

Health was also a concern. *The Companion* noted that the "bicycle fever here and the yellow fever in the south both seem to be spreading. There are several cases of diphtheria in town, and our boys and girls are not allowed to do downtown. Up here we have a clean bill of health."

The campus preoccupation with bicycling was juxtaposed against newspaper editorials clamoring for war with Spain. Nesbitt Tate, the superintendent's son, served as a University of Minnesota cadet, and Editor James Smith wrote, "[Nesbitt] makes a fine looking soldier. When war breaks out with Spain, maybe he will volunteer to go down to Cuba and help the patriots on that island gain their independence."

Esten didn't ease up academically. His first quarter grades in the Second Manual Class roughly equaled Bs, and for conduct, As. As for his progress as a printer, in one month of that school year, he scored perfect 100s for improvement and conduct and was never tardy.

During the bicycle and diphtheria rages, the boys stayed on campus and whiled away their hours playing rough-and-tumble football. The Minnesota School for the Deaf had a real coach this year, Louis Roth, a former student and Gallaudet College graduate. In November, the deaf school team lined up against Faribault High School, as twenty deaf school girls cheered from the sideline to inspire the determined boys. *The Companion* reported:

> Last Saturday afternoon the first football game ever played on our grounds with an outside team occurred, and resulted in a glorious victory for our boys. Their opponents were the Faribault High School eleven. The game was called at three o'clock. Our boys won the toss and chose the east goal. The high school kicked off, and the ball was caught and carried forward by our side. In the line-up a good advance was made, and the next time, the ball was passed to [Esten] Hanson, and aided by fine interference, he made a run of more than half the field and scored a touchdown. But referee Roth declared a foul, and the ball was brought back and given to the other side. They could not advance it, and lost it on downs. At the end of two twenty-five-minute halves, the score stood 26 to 0 in favor of the Minnesota School for the Deaf.
>
> Our boys then forced the fighting, and advanced steadily down the field, scoring their first touch-down in a few minutes. Goal failed. The remainder of the game was but a repetition of the first part. Our boys clearly outmatched the High School boys. Whenever the latter got the ball on a foul or fumble, they could not advance it through our line, and lost it on downs repeatedly. Nearly all the play was in

the opponents' territory, and at no time was our goal in danger. At the end of the first half the score was 16 to 0. It is due to the High School boys to say that they played a steady game throughout, and that although it must have appeared hopeless to them from the first, they played with even more determination during the second half than the first, preventing the scoring of more than ten additional points.

The playing on the part of our boys was characterized by fine team work and splendid interference. Our line was invincible, and no gains were made through it. The features of the game were the long runs made by [Esten] Hanson, the steady gains by Corbett, the tackling of Trost, and the success of Kucera in making gains through the line. Johnson at center played a cool and steady game, and in fact, all the boys deserved praise. Aside from a few fumbles, the game was free from errors, and these were excusable in a first game. The success of our boys was due chiefly to the excellent coaching of Mr. Roth, who gave them freely from his experience on many a well-fought field in the east.

Esten played left halfback and must have been fleet of foot and tough as nails to break free from tacklers and accomplish several long runs. Amazingly, after revealing so much latent talent, this turned out to be Esten Hanson's first, and last, organized football game.

Superintendant Tate—the sports-friendly Tate—soon gave an ultimatum: No more football match games unless all the players receive parental permission because of the many injuries. Football equipment and padding was quite minimal, and the game and the rules were still evolving, which could have led to Tate's decision.

Wrote Editor James Smith: "Football is receiving some opposition on account of the fatalities and serious accidents resulting from rough and reckless playing. Some place the game below pugilism, and our Iowa neighbor describes it as a term synonymous with barbarism. We do not look upon it in that light. There is no similarity between the pugilist and the football player. The intention of the former is to assault if not to mutilate; that of the latter, to play and win. The number of broken bones or calls for caskets do not decide the places of the two. We admit with regret that there have been more accidents than necessary from playing football, but the athletic associations are now modifying the rules of the game, and we hope the revision will be for the best."

Since his admittance, Esten had witnessed the student body, each year, become more and more interested in football and baseball, an interest that was becoming a tidal wave, and Esten was riding the crest. Having remained in Kerkhoven, he would not have had the same opportunity to play organized football—that sport would not reach Kerkhoven until 1908. As for baseball, Minnesota School for the Deaf students were playing organized baseball for years before anyone in Kerkhoven.

Masthead of *The Companion*, October, 1887, Esten's first year in school.
Courtesy of Minnesota State Academy for the Deaf, Faribault, Minnesota.

Esten Hanson, first-year pupil at the Minnesota School for the Deaf.
Edward Hoerger, Faribault, Minnesota, photographer. ca. 1887.
Courtesy Verna Johnson Gomer.

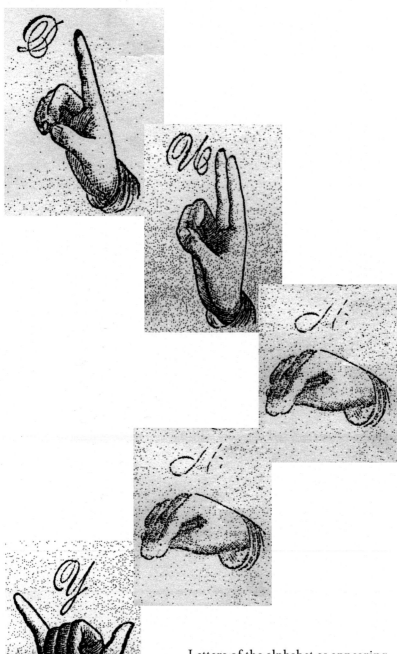

Letters of the alphabet as appearing
in *The Companion* on June 5, 1888.
*Microfilm Library, Minnesota State Academy
for the Deaf, Faribault, Minnesota.*

A Minnesota School for the Deaf baseball team. Esten Hanson is seated in the second row, far right. Other players are not identified. ca. 1892.
Courtesy of, and Esten's identification by Verna Johnson Gomer.

Picture upon which was based Esten Hanson's
written responses to questions spoken by his lip
reading teacher and his answers in 1893.
Minnesota State Historical Society Collections,
St. Paul, Minnesota.

WRITTEN WORK FOR

MINNESOTA EDUCATIONAL EXHIBIT

THE WORLD'S COLUMBIAN EXPOSITION

From School for the Deaf

Subject Questions on Picture. Lip-reading.

Executed by Esten Hanson   Age 10 Yrs.

How Prepared Copy of regular work

Time Occupied 30 Minutes   March F.   189 3.

Congenital deaf   In articulation class 3½ yrs. ½ hr. daily.

1. How many children do you see in the picture?
I see two children.

2. Who is with them?
Father.

3. What is the little girl doing?
She is looking at an owl.

4. Where is the owl?
The owl is sitting on a tree.

5. Are there the leaves on the tree?
No.

6. Do you think is in summer?
No.

7. Do you think is in the day time?
No.

8. Why do you not think so?
Because the moon is shining.

9. Which is large the boy or the girl?
The girl.

10. Is the window open?
No.

Esten Hanson's handwritten work product from his
1893 lip reading class.
Minnesota State Historical Society Collections, St. Paul, Minnesota.

Sunburg, Minnesota baseball team, June 16, 1894, the summer following Esten Hanson's seventh year at the deaf school. First published by the *Willmar Weekly Tribune*, Esten Hanson is identified in the picture as "Osten Sagedahl," standing at the far left. His brother, identified as "Hans (Hanson) Sagedahl," is seated on the far left.

Minnesota Historical Society Collections, St. Paul, Minnesota.

Photograph of Tosten and Betsy Hanson family and the
new Hanson farm home. L to R: Sons Hans Hanson, Julius
Hanson, and Esten Hanson. Seated are Tosten Hanson and
Betsy Hanson, his wife, and standing, son Bernt Hanson.
Daughters Ida and Sarah are seated on the railing of the upper
level porch; daughters Caroline (L) and Olina (R) are seated
on the lower level porch railing. ca. 1901.
Courtesy of, and identification by Verna Johnson Gomer.

1903 Kerkhoven, Minnesota Baseball Team: Top row, L to R: Frank Johnson, third base; Henry Gordhamer, infielder; Algot Westerdahl, Manager; Henry Johnson, first base (Captain and Treasurer); Johnny Johnson, second base. Middle row, L to R: Roy Hubbard, left field; Esten "Dummy" Hanson, pitcher; Carl Olson, Mascot; Oliver "Happy" Gordhamer, catcher; Raymond Cox, center field (Secretary). Front row, L to R: Henry Mahoney, shortstop–pitcher; and Bert Olson, right field.
Courtesy of Myrtice Gordhamer.

1904 Kerkhoven, Minnesota Baseball Team: Top row, L to R: Henry
Johnson, first base (Treasurer); Bob Hamon, Manager; Bert Olson, right
field; George Gordhamer; Roy Hubbard, left field. Middle row, L to R: Tom
Riffe, pitcher; Oliver "Happy" Gordhamer, catcher; Al Turner, second base.
Front row, L to R: Raymond Cox, center field-pitcher, (Secretary);
Esten "Dummy" Hanson, pitcher; Pete Storaker, position unknown;
Henry Mahoney, shortstop–pitcher.
Courtesy of Myrtice Gordhamer.

Photograph originally published in *The Kerkhoven Banner* on August 27, 1948. Caption identifies those pictured as: Back row, L to R: "Dummy" Hanson and Bob Hammond (sic). Seated, L to R: Al Turner, Bert Olson, Tommy Riffe, Dr. Grey, and George Gordhamer. Front row, L to R: "a Mr. Hubbard," Henry Mahoney, O. C. (Happy) Gordhamer, and Ford Pritchard. The caption also called attention to the turtle neck sweater worn by Esten Hanson. ca. 1904.
Minnesota Historical Society Collections, St. Paul, Minnesota.

Souvenir photograph of Boston Bloomers Baseball Team
which played the Kerkhoven baseball team on June 9, 1904 at
Kerkhoven, Minnesota. *Author's collection.*

INTERESTED SPECTATORS
AT
OREGON BALL PARK
5-3-'08
BOSTON BLOOMER GIRLS

Photograph marking occasion when the Boston Bloomer
Girls played at Oregon, WI on May 3, 1908. Shown here for
purposes of depicting the type of "canvas fence" described
in *The Kerkhoven Banner* on June 3, 1904 in promotion of the
Bloomers appearance in Kerkhoven, Minnesota on June 9,
1904. *Courtesy of Florine Paulson.*

Photograph of the May 3, 1908 Boston Ladies Base Ball Club
which played in Oregon, WI, shown here for purposes of
depicting the type of "private palace car" in which the team
traveled, as also described in *The Kerkhoven Banner* on June 3, 1904.
Courtesy of Florine Paulson.

Esten Hanson's official Death Certificate, dated September 20, 1908.
Note: Esten was not given a middle name or initial at birth; his correct and
full birth date was actually October 15, 1877.
Courtesy of the North Dakota Department of Health, Division of Vital Records, Bismarck, ND.

Photo of author's grandfather, Henry Johnson, at bat in July 4, 1910 game with the Benson, Minnesota team. Now shown to depict the close proximity of baseball fans to the action, common during this era.
Photograph by Charles Lincoln Merryman, photographer, Kerkhoven, Minnesota.
Author's collection.

The author assuming a batter's stance, as instructed
by his unseen grandfather, Henry Johnson. ca. 1937.
Author's collection.

CHAPTER TWELVE

HONORABLY DISCHARGED

A flood of tragic events around Thanksgiving 1897 affected Esten and others at the school. For one, a daughter of Judge Mott—the commissioner who appointed Noyes in 1866—Millicent Mott West, became terminally ill. Her sister, Alice Mott, who had been the school's art teacher from 1887 to 1894, had to hurriedly rush home from her studies at Yale University to be at her bedside. Millicent Mott West died on her father's seventy-second birthday, December 6, and the blow hurt not just Minnesota School for the Deaf, Judge ___ her seven children, but also all of Faribault. West's ___ s a University of Minnesota professor and ___ 'bault public schools. Weeks later, Judge ___ Caroline Hanson, to be his house servant. ___ rk for the deaf school. To secure employ- ___ ected Faribault family was a feather in her cap, and Esten's.

Ten days after Millicent Mott's death, the school was directly affected by the serious illness of the popular teacher and long-time *Companion* editor, James Smith, a widower since 1894 who was raising three children. He had alluded to physical problems in his December 16, 1897, news column, saying he had, "succumbed to the fates and the weather and is at present laid low with an attack of fever and ague. His many friends hope most sincerely that he will soon be again about his work, and crack jokes, as usual. This week's page of locals has been prepared by alien hands." The next week, he fought off a campus rumor of his having pneumonia. In a surprise New Year's Eve announcement, the new local physician, Dr. Robilliard, diagnosed Smith with malarial fever. Smith announced, optimistically, that he would be unable to resume teaching duties for at least a couple of weeks.

The School for the Deaf didn't exist in a vacuum. *The Companion* edition mentioning Smith's physical woes was mailed around the nation to other schools for the deaf. This brought written tributes from deaf schools in Pennsylvania, North Dakota, Texas, and others, as the closely knit Faribault deaf community rallied around its teacher, editor, and friend. One caring instructor shepherded her entire class to Smith's bedroom window, and they cheered him on using sign language. Good news erupted in mid-January, when Smith was finally able to leave his bedroom and hobble downstairs for a cup of hot tea. Smith wrote later that he had most likely contracted malaria on a horse and buggy trip through the wilds of northwestern Wisconsin.

The woods and swamps were filled with myriads of mosquitoes that flew about singing happily and working their profession for twenty-five hours a day. Our to [the writer and his companion] killed several millions, but there are still a few left to amuse the next explorers.

In spite of everything, the trip was regarded by our friends as a lark. But it seemed that there were other kinds of birds flying around, in the form of malarial microbes, and an undeniable number of those nested in the editor's anatomy and bided their time. This arrived in the fore part of December. The microbes woke up. They took right hold of the editor and gave him three awful shakings up, at regular intervals for three days. He paid no attention to this but went right on with his work. Then they took him by the neck and laid him on his back for four weeks' siege of malaria. Satisfied with their work, they then left him, and he is on his feet again, minus thirty-five pounds of avoirdupois.

Some of Smith's friends had questioned Dr. Robilliard's medical competency, believing they had known better. Smith put to bed most of those doubts when he publicly defended his doctor.

The month of February brought Valentine's Day, which was observed by the pupils and commented upon by the school's paper: "A good many valentines passed among the pupils, Monday. Some of the boys thought to have some fun by sending certain of the girls comic valentines, and they chose the most vulgar ones they could find in the stores. It was not a gentlemanly thing to do. The girls took it goodnaturedly, however."

Later that month, a group of boys ice skated on Klemer's mill-pond and strolled through downtown. In mid-March, Editor James Smith began reminding readers of another baseball season. Perhaps due to his weakened physical condition or his reluctance writing about temporal matters after facing death, he provided hardly any information about Esten's final year on the diamond, mentioning baseball in depth only once.

The sole account read,

There have been several games of baseball since our last issue. Our boys played a five-inning game with Shattuck last week Wednesday and were beaten, 7 to 6. On Friday afternoon they played a similar game on our grounds with a picked nine from town, winning 11 to 5. On Saturday afternoon they met the Voodoo nine, and were quite badly beaten, 24 to 3. The Voodoos were either heavy batters, or Pitcher [Esten] Hanson was not in good form, for the visitors had no difficulty in finding the ball and sending it all over the field. On the contrary, our boys made few safe hits. It does seem as if we are too weak at the bat. On Monday afternoon we had another short game with Shattuck on their grounds, and won by 6 to 2. We have a pretty good nine this year, and with a little more practice better playing will doubtless be seen. It is too early in the season yet to pass judgment. In fact, several of the players are still on trial in their positions. Our team is particularly strong in the battery and at second base. We would back Corbett against any catcher in Faribault, and he can make as pretty a throw to second as we have seen.

While suggesting the Voodoos slapped Esten around, Smith also patted him on the back when he commented on the battery, which referred to Esten and Corbett. The final reference to Esten's baseball career in Faribault appeared on April 21, when the Stars and Esten squeaked past Shattuck 5-2 in a four-inning affair. It must have been a somewhat satisfying finale to a graduating student who viewed Shattuck as his primary sports rival.

But the citizens of Faribault had priorities other than baseball, such as the Spanish-American War. Esten and his schoolmates should have been prime candidates for the U.S. military machine—except for one detail: they were deaf. The students showed their patriotic pride in late April by participating in parades and send-offs for the brave men marching to heed President McKinley's call for 725,000 volunteers. Faribault's Major George Whiting commanded one of Minnesota's regiments, volunteers marched to the railroad depot, and Faribault organized a patriotic rally. The Shattuck cadets double-timed around the deaf school grounds and St. Mary's. Several smaller deaf boys high-stepped behind them, waving their own American flags.

When Superintendant Tate raised the American flag on Saturday afternoon, people could see the cottony red, white, and blue flag flying from a mile away, the symbol of their freedom.

Amidst this, Esten graduated from the School for the Deaf, having been transformed over a ten-year period from an illiterate farm boy to a responsible man.

In mid-May, the school held its annual picnic. Esten probably saved the printed program as a school souvenir—as a printing student, he would have helped to produce it. He and his fellow students journeyed by carriage and foot to the abandoned grounds of the Tepee-Tonka Club on Cannon Lake, on a mild spring day, where the picnic would cast precious final memories of their school. The 230 students present enjoyed swinging, bicycle riding, flower picking, playing quoits, boating, and fishing, the latter the boys' favorite. The picnic committee provided spoon hooks. Many of the boys brought their own fishing tackle, and the shoreline remained occupied with boys all afternoon trying to "tempt the finny creatures from the lake water."

In a ball-throwing competition, baseball teammates Frederick Von Rueden, George Corbett, and Matthew Mies placed first, second, and third. At first glance, it seems puzzling that Esten would not have competed and placed, but perhaps distance throwing wasn't Esten's forte, or he was busy fishing for walleye. After all, pitchers and outfielders developed completely different skills and different muscles for throwing. A pitcher only needs to toss a baseball sixty feet or so; an outfielder must be able to hurl the ball three or four times farther.

The Minnesota School for the Deaf held commencement exercises on May 31, and present—undoubtedly smiling broadly—was twenty-three year-old Caroline Hanson, who had the unique opportunity to hear her employer, Judge Rodney Mott, speak and to witness her younger brother Esten finally finish school. As a proud sister, she had sacrificed a bit of her life and personal resources to see her deaf brother through. As Judge Mott offered practical advice, Caroline probably wiped tears of joy from her cheek, at this fulfillment of her dreams, and prayers, as she remembered their personal milestones together.

If only her family could witness the ceremony, except they had chosen to spend the time preparing for the continuation of a Syttende Mai celebration at home. It would have been grand had they the time, financial resources, and the desire, to visit Faribault. In the process, her parents could have visited their old stomping grounds—they had lived near Faribault at one time—and greeted their distant relatives. As Caroline listened, the Episcopal priest exhorted the graduates to "adopt some settled purpose and adhere to it with unwavering persistence."

GRADUATES
George Washington Corbett, Georgetown, Clay Co.
Gilbert Erickson, Wall Lake, Otter Tail Co.
Ellen Maude Graves, St. Paul, Ramsey Co.
Fannie Gunnarson, Minneapolis, Hennepin Co.
Frank Phillips, Bird Island, Renville Co.
Annie Saterland, Walbo, Isanti Co.
Victor R. Spence, Valley Creek, Washington Co.
Edna Louisa Vandegrift, Austin, Mower Co.

HONORABLY DISCHARGED
Esten Thosten Hanson, Sunburgh, Kandiyohi Co.
William Peters, Faribault, Rice Co.
Frederick Von Rueden, Faribault, Rice Co.
John Ernest Witt, Minneapolis, Hennepin Co.
Mary H. Witt, Goodhue, Goodhue Co.

The school honorably discharged, rather than officially graduated, Esten. Even though he had above-average grades, he had been part of the Second Manual Class, and all the graduates were in the First Manual Class. The designation didn't matter. The

School for the Deaf had taught him enough to succeed in the hearing world, official graduate or not. Providing a lasting memory, Superintendant Tate asked student Annie Normandin to recite in sign language two verses of *America*, inviting the audience to join in with their robust voices, while the School for the Feeble-Minded band accompanied. The song was a reminder of the country's ongoing war effort.

As Kerkhoven waited for his arrival, Esten couldn't get out of Faribault fast enough to start another summer of baseball. The new newspaper, *The Kerkhoven Banner*, mentioned that "Esten Hanson is expected home pretty soon. He graduated from the deaf and dumb institute in Faribault some days ago." In another article, the paper mentioned the error-prone Norway Lake ball players needing "bushel baskets" to improve faulty fielding. If holding to character, Esten had his eyes set on baseball, though his daily routine on the farm that summer would include feeding and milking the cows, hand-cranking the separator to remove cream from the milk, and feeding and watering the horses, pigs, and chickens. The work would be monotonous and tiresome. These would have to wait: his talented right arm—his primary means of self-expression—and the catcher's glove—his canvas.

CHAPTER THIRTEEN

COW PASTURE BASEBALL

Esten no longer had the Minnesota School for the Deaf and its baseball team as mentors. He now faced a life without them. School was done, forever finished. At the family farm, amid the cow moos, horse neighs, chicken clucks, and pig oinks, Esten Hanson heard absolutely nothing, as always, except possibly the dinner bell. To pursue his dream of pitching professionally, he had learned only one course of action from his experience at Minnesota School for the Deaf: patiently pay your dues until your peers have to take notice.

In 1898, Sunburg fielded a baseball team. According to the day's custom, towns sometimes hosted games involving out-of-town teams, such as *The Kerkhoven Banner* report in May 1898, noting that Swift Falls and Norway Lake had tangled "at the Sunburgh [sic] diamond last Sunday."

The Kerkhoven Banner (also referred to as *The Banner*) on July 31, *1898*, wrote of one such baseball game Esten could have been in: "A large crowd gathered in Hagen's grove, out near the Sunburgh [sic] store last Sunday to attend the harvest picnic. It had been advertised that the Terrace Brass Band and several speakers would be in attendance but for some reason all but one of the speakers and the band did not put in an appearance. The Quale boys sang several songs which were much appreciated by the crowd. The game of ball came off as advertised and was between the Norway Lake and Sunburgh nines. It resulted in a victory for the Norway Lake aggregation by a score of 13 to 6 and was a rather interesting game. No doubt the score would have been much larger had they had a good grounds on which to play!"

The town of Carlson began in late 1890 as a post office and the terminus of a biweekly stage route from Kerkhoven, eleven miles away. The first postmaster lent his name to the town, which was five miles west of the Hanson farm. The entire population of Carlson consisted of two unmarried men, who, between them, managed a blacksmith shop, a feed mill, a general store, and a post office. The closest doctor worked nine miles off. Though isolated in 1899, and small as a town could get, the men of Carlson had some hope of growth because telephone lines were spreading out over the prairie to revolutionize rural communication, psychologically closing the distances between towns. With the telephone, Carlson could become far less isolated, and more in touch with distant markets. The rumor going around was that a telephone line would soon extend from Norway Lake to Sunburg, thus keeping the Hansons more informed about life off the farm.

Western Minnesota seemed to be about five years behind Faribault in introducing fads; many town residents decided on making the bicycle a hot ticket that spring, right along with baseball. On April 7, 1899, Ben, the Western Hayes columnist in *The Banner* exhorted athletic young men in Hayes Township to form a baseball team, and a notice from Editor A. T. Archer two weeks later urged the young men of Kerkhoven to do likewise. Carlson chose to form two baseball teams. The two played each other in late April, with the winner acquiring the name, "Carlson High Kickers." Esten became a Carlson High Kicker. Esten's decision to join the Carlson team rather than the Sunburg or Kerkhoven teams was a simple matter: the Carlson post office was in the township of Kerkhoven and he was a resident of that township. His loyalty rested there— not with the hamlet of Sunburg or the village of Kerkhoven. In fact, the Carlson High Kickers scheduled Sunburg for its first game, although newspaper accounts don't record if the squads actually played.

Opposing columnists faced off in the May 19 Kerkhoven paper, with a columnist from "Midaros and vicinity" claiming the "regular" Carlson club had beaten the Carlson High Kickers, and then the Carlson columnist quickly put that rumor to rest, replying dead-pan, "The High Kickers defeated the Carlson baseball club last Sunday. Score 8-6." It wouldn't be the first or the last time local columnists had differing opinions over baseball in this newspaper.

Kerkhoven formed its baseball team in late May.

Hayes beat the Frank Lake team and scheduled a picnic and game on the Olaf Johnson farm in Hayes Township between the Carlson High Kickers and Murdock. No newspaper mentioned

Esten, but the score was indicative of his playing: Carlson 12, Murdock 5. Two weeks later, *The Banner* Sunburg columnist reported that the "Scandinavians" had won an ethnic tug-of-war over the Irish.

The July 4 celebration in Kerkhoven featured an outdoors Bowery dance as an added attraction, named after a type of dance cultured in the saloons and dance halls of the Bowery section of New York City. It was the kind of social affair the local Women's Christian Temperance Union (WCTU) chapter would not have approved. All the WCTU members must have smiled, though, upon hearing that the Bowery dance had not been popular, although the second dance was well attended, one for older adults, featuring Murdock's own Kelly Bros. Orchestra after the baseball game. The game had the Kerkhoven nine butting heads against the Carlson High Kickers, with the winners earning $25. Although having practiced a great deal, the Kerkhoven club hadn't played any games—so in that respect the High Kickers bore the advantage. However, Kerkhoven still had a healthy degree of self-confidence from having drubbed Benson the previous year. People flocked to Kerkhoven desiring to see the deaf boy in his inaugural appearance.

Since the newspaper build-up had been intense, *The Banner* tried making some sense for confused readers of the lopsided final: "The ball game between the Carlson and Kerkhoven clubs resulted in a victory for the Kerkhoven aggregation by a score of 18 to 2. The fact that the regular battery of the Carlson club was not here was undoubtedly the reason our boys run up so many scores. Only five innings were played."

Where was Esten? The *Swift County Monitor* explained the missing battery question, at least to a point, when reporting that Esten's catcher, Charles Magnuson, had recently contracted typhoid fever.

Esten could have refused to pitch without his security blanket. A few days later, a number of Kerkhoven townspeople picnicked at the Hanson farm on Monson Lake, and it would not have been surprising if some of the visitors teased Esten for not showing up for the big game. He could read lips, after all.

Grinding out the rest of the 1899 season, Hayes Township tripped up Danielson by scores of 38-23 and 37-9. The final newspaper mention of baseball that year came when the Hayes columnist, remembering the July 4 contest in Kerkhoven, remarked, "It would be interesting to witness another ball game between Kerkhoven and the [Carlson High Kickers]."

In Swift County, tobacco chewing and alcohol consumption had made significant inroads into the baseball scene—though Esten disapproved.

Kerkhoven WCTU members must have gasped when reading newspaper gossip about the number of brown jugs of liquor slyly brought into Sunburg to "hypnotize" the locals for Christmas celebrations. Perhaps a few of them were even preparing for the end of the world at the turn of the century, on January 1, as some fearful Americans had predicted. Locals knew the Hansons as fun-loving and hospitable, and guests may have brought liquor over to their home for the annual Syttende Mai celebrations. However, given his moral upbringing in Faribault, Esten would have frowned on alcohol usage, and he probably wished his mother would give up smoking a pipe.

The winter of 1899–1900 was Esten's second since leaving Faribault, but he was not oblivious to news outside of Swift County,

Minnesota. His school friend, Anthony Lykken, was a letter writer, and the Kerkhoven and Benson newspapers kept their readers current on happenings in the world, including the professional ranks of baseball. Reading news sheets, he would have become aware of the emergence of the new American League, comprised of cities located, at least in his mind, light years away from his Kerkhoven Township. Baseball players, such as Esten, dreamed of baseball greatness—he was very much aware of the achievements of "Dummy" Hoy, a deaf outfielder. He also knew that it was better to be a big fish in a small pond, rather than a small fish in a big pond. Closer to home, he knew that serious talks of organizing a ball team were taking place at the post office in Carlson, and that if he joined the team, he would have a battery mate who could handle his pitches. But first things first: the pasture ball fields had to lose their snow and mud while he bided his time working on the farm, ice fishing, and trapping muskrats and mink.

The year 1900 saw prairie baseball journalism become an art form, as dueling journalists competed in step with the tobacco- and alcohol-fueled teams they covered. The various teams, and journalists, awoke from that barren winter as hungry bears searching for sweet honey. The *Swift County Monitor* Hayes correspondent proudly said its nine would be a team to be reckoned with, and the Carlson correspondent replied to the *Monitor* editor, "The Carlson ball club has organized and soon will start playing." The Mud Creek nine, the other Carlson team, "was going to bloom in new uniforms," promised its partisan columnist. Choosing Palm Sunday to organize, the Carlson High Kickers officially became known as The North Stars, a name not unlike the Stars of the Minnesota School for the Deaf. Rolleo Gronseth's pasture became their home field.

A *Swift County Monitor* columnist, unaware of the team name change, said confidently, "... the High Kickers intend licking the dickens out of the Hayes Sports in the near future."

Ben, the Western Hayes columnist, fanned the Hayes-North Star competitive flame when announcing a forthcoming "battle" between the squads in mid-May: "The Carlson club had better bring a hay rack load of bushel baskets with treble reinforced bottoms and some bats 16 inches wide by 16 feet long with them when they come next Sunday."

The Banner Editor Archer said his solemn duty as a professional journalist forced him to warn North Star fans: "Otto Nybakke was in town Monday for some lime which he said he was going to use to 'whitewash' the Carlson [North Stars]." Nybakke played for Hayes.

The Banner mentioned an upcoming Syttende Mai celebration at the Ole Ligaarden farm south of Sunburg, and the Sunburg columnist commented that the celebration, "promises to be a good one. Wonder if the Swede-Norwegian contest will be decided there?" Hayes had the Swedes; the North Stars were the Norwegians. In 1900, though Sweden still officially ruled Norway, a Norwegian independence movement was afoot, and the tension carried over to Minnesota, where Norwegians and Swedes settled apart. A Hayes and North Stars rivalry struck a loud nationalistic chord that transcended baseball.

On May 18, 1900, the Western Hayes columnist said, "The Carlson club just came over to practice up for the 17th last Sunday. Yes, to practice up in 'rag chawin' not ball playing and they practiced so much that all their lower jaws have been stiff since. One poor fellow has been so bad that he has not been able to eat anything but boiled milk which he has drawn through a rubber hose. The

Carlson club not only had their bushel baskets and big bats along when they came last Sunday but also two expert baseball players, a pitcher and a catcher. The pitcher holds the honor (?) of being able to pitch thirteen different curves and the catcher was imported from Wisconsin especially for the occasion. The Hayes club at first refused to play with them on the grounds that an agreement had been made before they accepted Carlson's challenge that no player on either side should furnish a substitute, but after a while gave them the privilege of using the hired catcher if they would use their own 'glass arm' for pitcher. This however, for some reason unknown to us, they refused to do and reloaded their hay rack and returned home. Probably they were afraid that the Hayes club would score too close to them, thus spoiling the great reputation they built up for themselves last Fourth of July."

Ben's final sentence referenced the High Kickers' drubbing in Kerkhoven on July 4, 1899, when the former played without the services of Esten and Charlie Magnuson. Since Esten and Charlie had been absent then, the Hayes Township team understandably considered them as hired guns or "ringers," because they had never seen them play.

To set the story straight, *The Banner's* Sunburg columnist sent this parting shot over the Hayes bow: "We noticed an item in the Banner from Western Hayes about the (North Stars). It stated that they hired a catcher and a pitcher for the game recently played with their great and good Hayes club, which we wish to state was an untruth. The pitcher is a young man born and raised on Sec. 36, town of Kerkhoven. His name is Esten Hanson Sagerdahl and he has been the pitcher for the Carlson nine since it was organized. The catcher is a man from Wisconsin who has been around Carlson for the past three years and was the first one to agitate organizing a nine here. He has belonged to the nine since it was organized so consequently could not have been hired especially for that or any other game. His name is Charles Magnuson. Hereafter we hope that Western Hayes man will stick closer to the truth."

In an ensuing game against Kerkhoven, the Hayes columnist blamed their failures then on female distractions and, in the language of the day, on heavy drinking on their team's part the night before. Kerkhoven Editor Archer had to bite down hard not to gloat, saying that "some of our boys" had traveled to Hayes and "did that ball club" by a score of 12-4 over a shortened four innings. He added another subtle jab, "For further particulars see what our Hayes correspondent has to say."

News media trash-talking, innuendo, and speculation had, by now, crossed the mighty Rubicon, and so soon would player behavior. In a contest between Benson and Hancock, in which the visitors won, 17-7, the Hancock pitcher physically assaulted the Benson third baseman following a successful Benson double play in the seventh inning.

In late June, more sarcasm from the Kerkhoven editor: "An alleged ball game between the Hayes first nine and the Kerkhoven second nine was played on the Kerkhoven grounds last Sunday afternoon. Although only five innings were played the score ran up so high we haven't sufficient figures to give it. It was also very uneven in favor of the Kerkhoven club. As we don't like to hurt the feelings of any of the players we won't give the game an extensive writeup. If we told the truth, the whole truth and nothing but the truth about it we're afraid we wouldn't be able to get out a paper next week. A return game will be played on the Hayes grounds in the afternoon of July 1st, when it is hoped the boys will do better."

While shying away earlier, Hayes agreed to play the North Stars again, and lost, predictably, 20-3, at least according to the Sunburg columnist. The Western Hayes columnist shot back, protesting the game had never taken place. Ben said, "Now we are a member of the Hayes club ourselves and neither the captain or ourself ever heard of a game being played between those two clubs. We hereby wish to ask that rubber-necked [Sunburg columnist] with the merry-go-round head to keep his nose out of Town of Hayes business and try to tend to his own a little better hereafter."

The two squads played on July 4, with the North Stars soundly defeating the trash-talking Hayes squad, 11-3. Days later, Esten was the life of the party when his family hosted an after-party featuring early morning dancing, because he had led the Norwegians to sweet victory over the Swedes. The North Stars' lone loss that summer occurred in early August when they dropped a game to the Camp Lake Clippers. As if not believing Esten had been for real on July 4 against Hayes, another columnist, this one using the pen name of "Uncle Ola," again mentioned the possibility of Esten being a ringer. Talk of Esten's amazing talent spread further when he and the North Stars paid back the stubborn Camp Lake Clippers 6-2.

In early September, the North Stars and Hayes tangled again. The Sunburg columnist wrote: "The Carlson and Hayes clubs played a game of ball last Sunday. The Hayes boys were beaten so badly our modesty forbids us giving the score."

The area had one final game that season, a bragging-rights exhibition between the Hayes Republicans and Democrats, probably because someone from Hayes wanted to beat somebody—

anybody—before winter. With the contest held two weeks before an election, the Democrats, referring to themselves as the "Silver-ites," promised to defeat the "Gold Bug" Republicans by a score of 16-1. Newspapers have no record of the result. The terms "Silverite" and "Gold Bug" referred to President McKinley signing into law the Gold Standard Act of 1900, which struck down silver as a standard for redeeming paper money and established gold.

Esten's brother Hans, a bachelor, and Hans' friend Knute, left home the week before Thanksgiving to chop wood up north for extra money, a common winter practice for area farmers. At Hans' leaving, for an entire month, Esten became the oldest son at home, his having just turned twenty-three. Brothers Bernt and Julius were nineteen and sixteen, respectively.

Thanksgiving marked the beginning of the winter holiday season, and in the Hanson household that meant mouthwatering aromas, sights, and tastes of traditional Norwegian food. It was also a time to give thanks to God for their making it through another year. The Hanson dinner tables were filled with meat, fowl, breads, pastries, and home-grown vegetables. Everything except a cow's moo and a pig's oink were used—nothing of the butchered animals went to waste. The measure of a good cook was in how many types of cookies she baked for the day. After dinner, the men adjourned to the front room for discussion, and the women to the dishes.

Everything should have been right with Esten's world that Thanksgiving, and would have been, had he and his baseball playing associates not been reminded of life's fragility. All Esten could do was shake his head.

Esten's neighbor, Gustaf Finstad, had been a year younger, lived only a mile away, and had attended church with Esten. The manner in which Gustaf died confirmed in Esten everything Dr. Noyes had preached about demon alcohol. The Finstad family held the funeral on Thanksgiving morning and headed a caravan of forty-three wagons to the Norwegian church cemetery.

The Banner described the scene:

> Gustaf Finstad, a young man about 22 years of age, was found dead along side of the road about one mile east of the Swift Falls mill last Saturday morning. The dead man was the son of C. J. Finstad, of Sunburgh [sic]. Last Friday morning he went to Swift Falls for some flour and feed. He remained in Swift Falls until about six o'clock when he started for home. During the day he and several friends had bought and drank several bottles of DeWet's Stomach Bitters, which we understand a blacksmith at this place is selling as a substitute for whiskey. It seems that after starting home young Finstad became very sick from the effects of the stuff he had drank and fell from his wagon. He was so sick he was unable to help himself and laid where he fell until he died of exposure. When found about 11 o'clock Saturday morning life was extinct. The legs, arms and other parts of the body were frozen. After the driver fell from the wagon, the team turned around and returned to Swift Falls where they were found next morning standing

in front of the mill. The boy had been vomiting before falling from his wagon as the sacks on which he had been riding and his clothing were badly besmirched. Dr. Dowswell [a physician in Kerkhoven village] was called out Sunday evening to hold a post mortem examination and reports that death was caused by exposure. If there is any law that will reach the man who sold young Finstad the bitters, he should be punished. Deceased was an industrious young man and was well liked in the community in which he lived. His great failing was his love for strong drink. His relatives have the sympathy of all in their sad affliction.

The story made quick gossip fodder because the Swift Falls blacksmith, who was rumored to be a heavy drinker, more than likely, had been the same blacksmith operating in Carlson only the year before. News of other area alcohol abuse appeared that week in the *Swift County Monitor*, which published, under Kerkhoven Township news, the strident plea, "X-mas jugs are all the talk. Say boys, we wish you would pass one X-mas without a little brown jug." In the same issue, *The Banner* published a story of a dance until four in the morning at Knut Lien's place—on the same night Dr. Dowswell performed the autopsy.

That Sunday at church, pews and pews of people had drawn faces. The Hayes man first discovering the body believed that Gustaf had vacated the wagon to seek shelter in a nearby farmhouse before he passed out. He found a half-empty bottle of bitters in Finstad's pocket. The blacksmith selling the bitters immediately

fled the county—and the Hayes man carried home the tragic story
of the young farmer from Kerkhoven Township.

CHAPTER FOURTEEN

A FIELD OF HIS OWN

The early months of 1901 emphasized human mortality. Queen Victoria, who had reigned over the burgeoning British Empire sixty-three years, passed away in January. An assassin nearly finished off Wilhelm II, the German Emperor and Prussian King, who later pushed Germany into World War I. At home, the United States had two major typhoid outbreaks, the Great Fire of 1901 wiped out Jacksonville, Florida, and for the first time, the U.S. stock market crashed. It was all foreign news to Esten, whose world consisted almost entirely of summer pasture baseball and farm chores. Outside news seldom drifted his way, except for the everyday gossip of the people of Kerkhoven (population 411), Murdock (275), DeGraff (165), and Benson (1,525).

The North Stars' 1901 baseball schedule originally listed eleven games against five teams: Hayes, Norway Lake, Grace-Havelock of

Chippewa County, Kerkhoven, and an unidentified all-star team. Newspaper accounts recorded at least four rain-outs and only four games played, with two games appearing at a newly crowned venue: Tosten Hanson's pasture on the northeast shore of Monson Lake, across the wagon trail from the new Hanson residence. A ball field would tie in masterfully with the soon-to-be recurring picnics and dances at Tosten's fashionable place and the always-present dog-days flow of sun worshipers frequenting Monson Lake.

Preparing the ball field for season play was Esten's delight, i.e., filling in gopher holes and leveling other field bruises, clearing brush, hauling rocks, marking base paths, and measuring the distance from home to the pitching mound. Now all Betsy and Tosten had to do to watch Esten pitch was walk across the road—the ball field was almost in their front yard! It was his field of dreams, until a newspaper columnist brought out the hatchet against him and his teammates.

In early April, a *Kerkhoven Banner* Hayes Township columnist adopting the pseudonyms "U.S." and "U. S. and His Playmate," wrote: "The 'Povel' of Carlson, or rather what is known as the 'Carlson Povel' passed through here last Friday from Murdock to Carlson with a wagon load of bitters and J. T. tobacco which we understand he will feed to the Carlson ball players so that they will be ready for play whenever called upon."

In his one sentence, "U.S." had stepped on a sensitive nerve. He had publicly branded the North Stars as a bunch of tobacco-chewing, whiskey drinkers, and, in a backhanded sort of way, may have been commenting on the untimely death of Gustaf Finstad, still a delicate topic. That holier-than-thou attack would not have set well with the Norwegian Carlsonites, let alone Esten, who had been taught at the School for the Deaf to eschew tobacco and alcohol. Whether valid or not, the columnist's choice words must have stung as hard as an errant fastball to the rib cage.

The Sunburg columnist replied a week later: "If U. S. expects to beat those Carlson ball players this season he had better get at them before they consume much of that load of bitters and J. T. Tobacco."

Another neighborhood columnist chimed in, "U. S. had better gather up his ball nine and play those Carlsonites before they get too much of the bitters and J. T."

The Carlson columnist piled on, "Who is the Carlson Povel? We don't know of anyone going by that appellation. The Hayes correspondent must have had the nightmare when he saw that being pass by."

The North Stars played their first game that season at Tosten Hanson's pasture baseball diamond in mid-April, but not against rival Hayes. *The Banner's* Kerkhoven Township writer, only in passing, mentioned the North Stars' early-season play that day, saying tongue-in-cheek, "The Carlson ball club played their first inning last Sunday but they had consumed too much J. T. Tobacco and Carlson bitters to make a very good showing."

A week later, the same writer tweaked Hayes again: "We wonder if the Hayesers will start up their ball nine and try the Carlson club this year. If they do they will have to go against that imported shorthorn stock again." The last reference was to catcher Charles Magnuson, who had the ideal physical attributes of a catcher.

Sunburg was becoming a rockin' town. Along with Tosten's dances, picnics, and baseball games, the local general store celebrated a grand opening by sponsoring a dance that lasted until four in the morning. Some Hayes players attended, which sparked this comment from the Hayes writer, "If the Carlson club can't handle all of the J. T. the Hayes boys will take some, but they don't want any bitters."

By May 1, Hayes and the North Stars still hadn't butted heads. After the Hayes columnist mentioned the North Stars' alleged drinking and chewing habits yet one more time, the Sunburg reporter, tiring of the worn mantra, answered, "The Hayes ball players lack backbone. The Carlson team has gone to the Hayesers grounds twice but the latter refused to play both times."

Hayes responded: "The bitters which was taken to Carlson some time ago is reported as being 'bad' medicine."

The next week, the Hayes correspondent, said, "We have neither the reason nor desire to hurt the feelings of any of the Carlson ball club but as [their] correspondent is getting a little ridiculous we will have to straighten him out a bit. We have played the Carlson club twice. Once at Eric Paulson's place, and last 4th of July at Monson Lake. At the first mentioned game they played their six best men and picked the three best players out of the West Lake club and we beat them without having to bat our last half inning. At the latter place they hired Mr. O. Torgerson, the Sunburgh [sic] pitcher, to pitch for them. The [Sunburg] Story Teller had better ... let the Hayes ball club alone."

Of course, the two games noted, played at Eric Paulson's place and at Monson Lake, occurred in June and July of 1900, the year before.

To which *The Banner's* Sunburg correspondent replied: "Ben [the Hayes correspondent] misrepresented things last week when he said the Hayes ball club has beat the Carlson club. The Carlson nine did not play the Hayes nine at Eric Paulson's place. It was the West Lake and Hayes clubs that played there. A few of the Carlson players played with the West Lake boys. The reason Olai Torgerson pitched for the Carlson club at the game played last 4th of July was because some of the Hayes players objected to the regular pitcher, Esten Hanson, being allowed to pitch and Torgerson took his place. Hereafter you should not misrepresent things Ben, as you make yourself unpopular by doing so."

Baseball was changing. After the American League began in 1901, the National League, feeling competitive heat, changed its rules to speed up the game and make it more spectator-friendly. For instance, the pitcher had to throw his first toss within twenty seconds after a batter entered the box; a batter hit by a pitched ball could not take first base, but only added a "ball" to his pitch count; and the catcher had to stand less than ten feet behind the plate and batter. Readers of *The Banner* knew of the National League rule changes, and local umpires may have adopted some.

As for Esten, and the Carlson North Stars, any rule changes didn't affect their success, as they steamrolled over and through area opponents. After whipping the Norway Lake team 7-2 at the annual May 17 Syttende Mai celebration, the Carlson team, speaking as one in the *Swift County Monitor*, confidently challenged "any nine this side of Minneapolis" to a game of baseball. The reporter added this about Esten: "The Carlson ball pitcher has improved his arm with some arrangement that we cannot give any name. It is kind of an automatic arm, so it works easy to throw the ball."

At this stage in his career, twenty-three-year-old Esten Hanson was a dominating pitcher capable of throwing fastballs and curves, and, given his ability to keep opponents' scores low, pitching under control. Any modern baseball fan worth his or her salt realizes that a pitcher's ability to consistently throw strikes determines his ultimate effectiveness. It appeared that Esten enjoyed showing off his "automatic" arm.

In the absence of any worthy opponent that spring, the Carlson North Stars arranged to tangle with an "All-Star" team consisting of the best diamond men from Hayes, Swift Falls, and Norway Lake. The game would be played on Tosten Hanson's ball diamond, and include a picnic and an open house for Tosten's recently built home, one of the largest in the vicinity. A week before, the Hansons had hosted a dance at their fifteen-room Victorian frame home, surrounded by a generous front porch held high by massive pillars, and now they would host a baseball game. In a photograph that could have been taken that Sunday, the entire Hanson family posed for the camera, with the lone exception being eldest daughter Isabelle, who had married in 1887 and lived elsewhere. Wearing their Sunday-best clothing, Tosten and Betsy posed in the forefront, with Esten directly to Tosten's right. Two other sons stood on the back porch, while daughters Caroline, Ida, Oline, and Sarah adorned the railings of the porches, one on each of the first and second stories, two daughters to a level. It must have been a grand moment for Tosten to document for posterity his large family and Victorian palace, especially after having experienced such trying financial times a few short years before. The family pride of that day must have left a lasting impression on Esten.

The Banner reported: "A picnic was held at Monson Lake Sunday. The principal feature was a game of ball between the Carlson club and a nine composed of some of the best players of the Hayes, Swift

Falls and Norway Lake clubs. It resulted in an easy victory for the Carlson boys by a score of 7 to 1. The Carlson club will play the Grace-Havelock club at this place on the Fourth for a purse of $50."

The Monson Lake correspondent: "The Carlson boys demonstrated that they could play ball last Sunday at the picnic. They came near shutting out the opposing club. The score was 7 to 1."

The Carlson North Stars juggernaut gained steam. After a practice game against a Kerkhoven club, in which the North Stars uncharacteristically lost 9-3, the North Stars were headed for a well-publicized July 4 game against Grace-Havelock over a $50 purse. Grace-Havelock hailed from Chippewa County. *The Banner's* account of that July 4 celebration included these words about the main attraction:

> Mother Nature decided to interfere and accordingly did what she usually does on the Fourth of July—favored us with a copious shower of rain. The crowd was left to its own devisement for entertainment until about 2:30 o'clock when an effort was made to pull off the ball game. Just as the boys were ready to commence the game, however, another shower, heavier than the first came up and drove the crowd back to town. No further effort was made at pulling off the sport until after 4 o'clock when the crowd reassembled at the ball ground to witness the game between the Havelock and Carlson clubs. It resulted in an easy victory for the Carlson aggregation by a score of 25 to 6. Although the game was one-sided it was sufficiently interesting to hold the crowd until it was completed and abounded with good plays and unpardonable errors. It was after 6 o'clock before the game was finished.

Fueled by their June 30 practice-game triumph over the North Stars, the Kerkhoven nine desperately sought a rematch to confirm their field prowess, but it was not meant to be. A mid-August game did not go off as scheduled at Tosten Hanson's pasture, and rain on September 6 washed out a match-up at Hayes between the North Stars and Kerkhoven.

So Esten Hanson's baseball season ended, and his father's harvest began. If not working for his father, he could have earned about two dollars a day as a field hand harvesting wheat that was fetching approximately fifty-six cents a bushel. Area farms yielded up to fifteen bushels per acre. With winter not far off, farmers began hauling firewood cut in the woods of Camp Lake and Norway Lake, and some, if time permitted, hunted prairie chickens and ducks. Esten remained in the stylish Victorian that fall, at least through Thanksgiving, when the Monson Lake reporter declared that, "Mr. Antonny Lykken of Goodhue County" had been Esten's guest. The two had been long-time friends at Minnesota School for the Deaf. Days earlier, the newspaper had reported that Lykken and Esten had visited Lue and Ed Evenson. Could Esten have been consulting with his close friends about the future of his baseball career?

CHAPTER FIFTEEN

EDEN VALLEY

"Esten Hanson, of Monson Lake, is now working in the *Banner* office. He is deaf and dumb and learned the printing business while attending school in Faribault," the March 21, 1902, *Kerkhoven Banner* described.

On the surface, at least, the idea of Esten as a *Banner* employee would have been a logical one, considering his extensive Minnesota School for the Deaf training. But there were likely more reasons. The Kerkhoven baseball team, after luckily pummeling the Carlson nine in a practice game and issuing a bold challenge to play any team within twenty-five miles, may have asked Editor Archer to provide a job for Esten. He could then pitch for Kerkhoven.

In the weeks after the surprise hiring, either Archer just had bad luck with his printing press or Esten committed some costly mental errors after having not worked one in almost four years. It was a fact that Esten was farsighted and had difficulty seeing close up. The April 4 edition noted that the newspaper had been several hours late the previous issue, which would have been Esten's first full week on the job, with the excuse being that the printing press had broken down.

Two weeks later, the press broke down again, this time causing a one-day delay. Archer said, "We do not believe that we will ever be called upon to apologize for being late on account of that particular part of our press breaking again, however, as we have had a new piece made by Blacksmith Mattson that is so strong it can't be broke."

Sometime after March 21—*The Banner* mentioned Esten in that issue—Esten suddenly quit his newspaper job and relocated to Minneapolis, and from then until mid-September the only authoritative news of his whereabouts originated from two *Kerkhoven Banner* articles. Both, in mid-September, mentioned Esten Hanson returning, with one reporting: "Mr. Esten Hanson returned from Eden Valley Thursday of last week [September 11] where he has been traveling around playing ball. He spent the first part of the summer in Minneapolis."

Why Eden Valley? Esten had probably gone to visit James O'Leary, a Minnesota School for the Deaf graduate from the class of 1890, who owned two weekly newspapers, including one in Eden Valley. O'leary, a former teammate of Ed Sampson, had been elected captain of the school's first teams in 1889.

The Companion confirmed in mid-November 1901 O'Leary's presence in Eden Valley: "We have just received copies of two newspapers in which Mr. J. H. O'Leary is interested. They are *The Eden Valley Journal* and the *Kimball Kodak*. Eden Valley and Kimball are two towns in Stearns County, not far apart. Mr. O'Leary goes back and forth between the two, attending to his twofold business. His family is established in Eden Valley, and it is there that he trots his son and heir on his knee after the labors of the day are over. This heir bears the name of James Halvorson O'Leary, and is therefore entitled to call himself J. H. O'Leary, Jr."

As for Esten staying in Minneapolis in early summer, his newlywed sister, Caroline, could have provided free room and board for him there. Officially, she married Norwegian native Christian Skeie on June 29, 1902, in Minneapolis. She certainly had been interested enough in his welfare to sacrifice for him years before—moving from Sunburg to Faribault. They were emotionally close. It would be almost impossible envisioning Esten moving to Minneapolis without his being at least somewhat familiar with his landlord.

It was common in the late 1800s for Minnesota School for the Deaf graduates to gravitate toward Minneapolis and St. Paul. *The Companion* reported extensively on the deaf community in the Twin Cities. Former first team players had organized a deaf baseball club in Minneapolis, which at one time had included Ed Sampson. "Hearing" baseball teams around the Twin Cities also occasionally hired deaf players.

In mid-May, *The Companion* announced, "Mr. Sarom Olson, of Minneapolis, was in Faribault last Saturday, calling on old friends and trying to arrange a ball game for the team composed of deaf boys of Minneapolis, of which he is the manager." As a second baseman on the 1896 first team featuring Esten as pitcher, Sarom could have been Esten's catalyst for leaving home for Minneapolis—sister Caroline may have been only the means. Notices in *The Companion* on two separate occasions emphasized the team's need for pitchers. It would have been understandable for Esten to quit his day job at *The Banner* to pursue one last summer of baseball with old friends.

While networking on that team, Esten could have learned through fellow alumnus James O'Leary of Eden Valley's pressing need for pitchers. Eden Valley was only forty miles east of Sunburg, a rural town of less than a thousand population, and much closer to home. O'Leary had friends in the Minneapolis deaf community, and he personally knew almost every player on the Minneapolis team. A mover and shaker over and above newspaper publishing, O'Leary became an elected delegate to the Meeker County Democratic convention that fall, even though he was deaf and mute. Eden Valley newspaper accounts of Esten pitching that summer would have been preserved for posterity had not O'Leary's entire printing plant been consumed by a roaring fire that fall. The *Litchfield Independent* reported the fire starting in a butcher shop next door, and that "nothing was saved, even the books and subscription list of the *Journal* being destroyed." In time, O'Leary moved to Seattle, Washington, to start a daily there.

Yet there were other newspapers. The *Litchfield Independent*, published thirteen miles from Eden Valley, announced a mid-June game between Litchfield and Eden Valley. The newspaper did not record the outcome. The *Dassel Anchor*, located thirty miles from Eden Valley, acknowledged a game in which Dassel defeated Eden Valley 4-3. The "Valleyite" pitcher, O'Brien, threw "slow benders" and a "slow ball that fooled the locals for a long time, all of the boys blazing away when the ball was scarcely half way to the plate."

During Litchfield's July 4 celebration, the team from Atwater knocked heads with Eden Valley. Given that July 4 was no longer "early summer," Esten probably had already arrived from Minneapolis. This *Dassel Anchor* newspaper account could have been speaking of him: "The Eden Valley and Dassel baseball teams as well as their friends and admirers, were treated to a surprise last Friday in the games for $100 at Litchfield. Atwater defeated Eden Valley in a close game of 4 and 3. The Valley boys had the game won up to the ninth when Atwater tied the score and a wild throw to third base by the Valley pitcher gave Atwater the game and the purse. Had the pitcher played for the batter the story might have been different ... Eden Valley should have won easily, but luck was also against them." Did Esten commit an error costing his team the game—and cash prize?

Two days later, the squads squared off in Dassel. The *Dassel Anchor* lifted coverage of the game verbatim from the *Eden Valley Journal*, a common practice in rural weeklies. This also left an example of James O'Leary's reporting. The *Dassel Anchor* described the scene: "The Eden Valley Journal has the following to say of us: 'The Eden Valley baseball team went to Dassel Sunday and played the strong Dassel team a close game that they would have won but for four unfortunate errors in the eighth inning that let in four scores. Eden Valley accumulated three all told and played an excellent game all around except in the fatal eighth. The boys reported excellent treatment and say they never met a finer aggregation of ball players and fans and never saw a squarer umpire than Ben Record. Dassel gave Eden Valley the credit of being the best team they met this season and said further that they never met more gentlemanly fellows.'"

Nothing more was recorded of Esten's 1902 baseball exploits.

In mid-September, Esten reviewed his experience of living in Minneapolis and playing ball for Eden Valley while visiting his good friend Lue Evenson, which *The Banner* faithfully reported.

CHAPTER SIXTEEN

SECRET ARRANGEMENT

The Swift County baseball scene survived Esten's absence, especially Kerkhoven, which had tasted enough diamond success to believe that 1903 could be much better with a star pitcher. Carlson and Sunburg squads competed, too, as did Norway Lake. If Esten, that winter, considered playing for Carlson or Sunburg in 1903, his dreams would have been crushed in December upon hearing that his battery mate, Charles Magnuson, had fallen from twenty-four-feet up while constructing a barn. On the way down he hit a 2x4 with his shoulder, which broke his fall, then landed on his head. It was a devastating injury to a catcher and a friend.

Perhaps seeing an opportunity, or maybe having been told of one, Oscar (O.T.) Carlson met with Esten in early February at Oscar's home five miles north of Kerkhoven. It would appear from all accounts that Esten approached Oscar first. Oscar and his brother, Albert, then went off to attend Metropolitan Business College in Minneapolis for a three-week course, and they returned home just in time for the election. Oscar was running for Constable of Hayes Township. When his father had died in 1891, Oscar Carlson suddenly had become the man of the house at the age of twelve, so he was used to shouldering responsibility.

In mid-March 1903, *The Banner* headline announced that the village of Kerkhoven had banned the sale of alcohol, yet again, by a 222-36 margin. The WCTU held sway this time in what seemed like a perpetual see-saw battle. The village had been dry in the early 1890s only to switch back a few years later. Following this vote, the blind piggers must have rejoiced, and with smiles on their faces and silently thanking the voters, began restocking their shelves for the anticipated demands by residents of Kerkhoven who wanted to wet their whistles. The momentum in much of Minnesota was moving toward temperance, as evidenced by the Kerkhoven vote, and that of other towns, and this from the Monson Lake reporter: "We are very much pleased to hear that the saloons had been voted out of Kerkhoven, and we do not think it will now be necessary to be dodging drunken men every time we go to town as we have been doing for several years past. You did right people of Kerkhoven, to vote them out, and we hope you'll keep them out."

Two weeks later, Esten met with his friend Lue Evenson, who he often consulted before major decisions. Esten could have been considering moving to Canada, and in doing so following a number of Swift County men. Canada had a superabundance of available rich farmland conducive to producing wheat. In fact, the migration of able-bodied men there had somewhat depleted the Hayes and Kerkhoven Township rosters that year, including that of the farm family hosting the Hayes home games, the Ole Nybakkes, whose eldest (age 25) son, Andrew, had established a homestead at Estevan, Saskatchewan, Canada, which he intended to occupy in the near future with his new bride.

The area baseball season began in earnest, when the Jack Creek nine sliced up Murdock, and the Chippewa County Smith squad defeated Louriston, 6-3. The Kerkhoven nine lacked motivation to organize, and so Editor Archer kept prodding. In late May, he chronicled this baseball game, the first for Kerkhoven, between that town's married men and Murdock's:

The married men's ball game scheduled to be played at Murdock last Sunday afternoon between clubs from Murdock and Kerkhoven did not materialize for the following reasons, to-wit: To strengthen their team the Murdockers secured a young married farmer, Frank McCann, to play with them. To offset this the Kerkhoven boys wished to play one of the young men of this village. The original agreement was that none other than resident married men should be allowed to play in either club. The manager of the Murdock team refused to play his club without the outsider alluded to and also refused to allow the Kerkhoven aggregation to play one of the young men. After 'heap big talk,' it was decided to call the married men's game off and arranged that a club composed of the best players that could be picked from the Kerkhoven crowd that had gone up to witness or participate in the game be pitted against the regular Murdock club. The game played was quite interesting and resulted in a victory for the Kerkhoven aggregation by a score of 12 to 17. J. S. McGovern, of Murdock, officiated as umpire and came in for the usual amount of criticism and abuse. A fair sized crowd was present to witness the game and expressed themselves as being well pleased with the ball playing, but thoroughly disgusted with those who devoted so much of their time to argument.

Competitive juices fueled Kerkhoven town pride. Editor Archer advertised a fundraising event that brought in $56.90. While all the players hadn't been selected, L. W. English was elected as manager, Henry Johnson as captain and treasurer, Raymond Cox as secretary, and Carl Olson was chosen to be the mascot. The team lacked a really good pitcher. Ray Cox was decent, but no giant killer. Henry Johnson could pitch in a pinch, but if he did, who would play first base? "Bottle" Berg would become great in time, but at only thirteen, he wasn't ready. Esten Hanson, the Carlson North Stars and Eden Valley ace, seemed a logical choice, especially given Esten's employment at *The Banner* the year before. Only one hurdle: Esten had been paid to play in Eden Valley and would expect pay in Kerkhoven.

Oscar Carlson, the Hayes catcher who purchased his farm supplies in Kerkhoven, traded with Ray Cox and Henry Johnson, the Kerkhoven team organizers who made their livings purchasing hogs and cattle from farmers and selling firewood and horses and operating a dray line, respectively. The families of ballplayers Bertie Olson and Oliver Gordhamer traded with the Carlsons, too. Around the time when the Kerkhoven team organized, the Monson Lake reporter mentioned that, "Esten Hanson called at Carlson's one day last week." The newspaper then declared that Esten and Oscar had gone to Kerkhoven to take in the scheduled May 24 contest between the married men of Kerkhoven and Murdock. The Murdock men canceled that game for lack of players.

Due to depleted rosters, previously warring Carlson and Hayes swallowed their competitive pride and decided around May 24 to form a united team. The combined squad, without Esten, scheduled a game against the Jack Creek team.

While riding together to Kerkhoven, on May 24, Esten and Oscar had far more on their minds than watching a relatively meaningless baseball game. In his next edition, Editor Archer revealed their trip's purpose: "We understand that an arrangement has been made whereby Esten Hanson, of Monson Lake, will play ball with the Kerkhoven club this summer. Esten is a good player and will materially strengthen the club." The "arrangement," a handshake agreement, meant Esten would receive pay. Although not publishing his salary, the newspaper did publish a figure in 1904 that was in line with what other players of similar ability earned. The *Swift County Monitor* Carlson correspondent subsequently lamented Esten playing ball for the Kerkhoven team.

May 30, 1903, Memorial Day, was to be Esten's first appearance in a Kerkhoven baseball uniform. On June 5, *The Banner* published its "Sunburg News" correspondent's recognition of that fact: "Esten Hanson went to Kerkhoven on his wheel last Saturday to pitch for the Kerkhoven ball team in a game they played with the Murdock team." Arriving and welcomed by his new teammates, he took batting practice and was warmed up by Kerkhoven's catcher, Oliver "Happy" Gordhamer, together having previously decided on the signals between them for Esten's various types of pitches.

Promptly at 2:30 p.m., the umpire called, "Play Ball!" and as the home team took the field, Esten quickly walked to the pitcher's mound and, placing his rear foot against the rubber slab, threw a few more easy pitches to Happy. Satisfied he was ready, and after glancing at each of his infielders, he turned and faced his first batter. Although his legs were tired out from pedaling his wheel over eleven miles of dirt roads from his farm home to Kerkhoven, he was adrenalized and ready to throw his first pitch against Kerkhoven archrival Murdock—as a paid ball player.

Editor Archer described the scene: "A very interesting game of ball was that played here last Saturday afternoon between the Murdock and home teams. The latter were victorious by a score of 9 to 16. At the commencement of the game it looked very much as though the lads from up the line were going to be victorious, as at the end of the second inning the score stood 8 to 2 in their favor. Thereafter, however, the locals did better work and not another Murdockite crossed home plate until the ninth inning when another score was added to their count. Our boys succeeded in scoring in nearly every inning and before the game ended were ahead by a very substantial margin. Unlike the game played at Murdock several weeks ago, this one was almost entirely devoid of disagreeable wrangling and the crowd that witnessed it was much better pleased. A large number of Murdock and country were here to witness the game."

At first, the Murdock boys must have smelled blood against this deaf and dumb Norwegian, and they no doubt hurled a number of normally effective verbal taunts, none of which Esten heard. He had nothing more than first game jitters and answered their early game barrage with a hitless blanking from the third through eighth innings. Near the end, their pathetic bats seemed to swing as rusty farm gates.

Esten's talent seemed to surprise everyone. He next mowed

down the cocky Louriston-Smith club 19-2. After the contest, Manager English resigned as club manager, citing lack of time, and A. Westerdahl, an early WCTU supporter, replaced him. The latter, in his thirties and a friend of Editor Archer, was a school board member, musician, and fraternal lodge brother.

Kerkhoven next played undefeated Raymond, and the Raymond newspaper filed this report:

> The Raymond baseball team accompanied by eight or ten rooters drove over to Kerkhoven Sunday and tried conclusions with the team of that place. They were defeated by a score of 19 to 7. The uneven score might suggest that the game was not a very interesting one but it was, however, and but for rank errors which were evidence of lack of practice and experience the game would have been very close. Both sides made plenty of errors but the home team suffered the most, as every error made cost them a score or two. Then too, the team was handicapped by the absence of Louis Johnson, the catcher, and his place was filled by Henry Jackson, who has not caught behind the bat for years but done exceptionally good work. Louis Herman pitched a splendid game but his support all around was weak. His good work can easily be realized from the fact that the ball was only knocked out of the diamond three times in the entire game and only one two-base hit was made by the opponents. The Kerkhoven team is composed of pretty good players all old heads and evenly matched, and play fairly well. The pitcher is a deaf and dumb mute, plays ball all the time and never says a word. While he throws ball pretty well he is not a phenomenon by any means and the boys found him for safe hits nearly every inning.

The team's first road trip involved their taking a horse and buggy, first, for a return match-up against Raymond, and next, against undefeated Clara City. Kerkhoven bested Raymond 13-10, and therefore earned the amateur bragging rights for that part of the state, wrote Archer. The next game, against Clara City, was a long-awaited rematch of the 19-11 drubbing Kerkhoven had received the previous year.

Compared to the *Raymond News* and *Chippewa County News*, Archer penned rather benign commentaries, this one about the Clara City game:

> Our club remained in Raymond Saturday night and the following day drove to Clara City and that afternoon crossed bats with Manager Yock's Colts, as the Clara City team is styled. This game also resulted in a victory for our boys by a score of 6 to 15. In company with several others, ye editor drove over to see the game and had the honor—or more properly speaking, the misfortune—of being selected to umpire the game. Our work was too coarse to suit the Clara City people, however, and they proceeded to 'kick' on some of our VERY FAIR decisions. The game was an exciting one, which was no doubt due in part to the fact that a large delegation of Raymondites were on hand to 'root' for Kerkhoven. This they did in a very satisfactory manner— from a Kerkhoven standpoint—although it seemed to have the effect of ruffling the temper of some of the Clara City players and 'rooters.' The best feature of the game was the pitching of Esten Hanson as at the end of the game he had no less than 15 strikeouts to his credit. The Clara City boys succeeded in scoring in only two innings, the first and the sixth, in each of which they made three runs. Although the

Clara City pitcher, Bell, was by no means an easy mark, our boys succeeded in finding the ball whenever they wanted to and had it been necessary could have run up a larger score than they did. Our team and those with them received courteous treatment at the hands of the Clara City people and we hope to be able to reciprocate when their team comes here to play the return game, which they will do shortly after the Fourth.

On June 26, the *Raymond News* reported on Kerkhoven's victories over Raymond on June 20 and Clara City on June 21, proclaiming, "THEY WIN BOTH GAMES." Of the Kerkhoven-Raymond game its editor wrote:

The Kerkhoven base ball team accompanied by a few rooters came down last Saturday and played the return game with the local team. The visitors carried off the honors by a score of 13 to 10. The game was full of errors and both sides played very poorly at different intervals throughout the game. The visitors were in the lead right from the start and the game was very one-sided until the sixth inning when the home team put on their batting clothes and scored six runs, making the score 9 and 11 in favor of the visitors. The visitors changed pitchers in the seventh inning, taking out Mahoney and putting the deaf and dumb twirler, Esten Hanson, in the box. The home team scored one in the seventh and should have easily tied the score in the ninth but for very careless base running. The visitors scored two in the eight giving them a total of 13. Herman and Johnson were the local battery and did good work but their support in spots was very weak.

In justice to the entire Kerkhoven team we wish to say they are all gentlemanly players and the game was played without any disputes or wrangling whatever. Both sides play friendly and clean ball and with such there is no excuse for any 'rag chewing.' Wm. Blake acted in the capacity of umpire and it goes without saying that the genial old 'has-been' still has a fond recollection of the rudiments of the game and is familiar with the rules from start to finish.

A base ball dance was given in honor of the visitors at the McKinley hall in the evening but as the Kerkhoven boys had to play another game the next day not many of them indulged. Those who did, however, report a very pleasant time.

The Kerkhoven boys speak in words of greatest praise of the treatment accorded them by the home team and the people of Raymond. They were given a royal welcome when they arrived in town and escorted to the hotel and made to feel in every way sociable. They left Sunday morning for Clara City, where they played the team of that place in the afternoon.

In that issue, the *Raymond News* also spoke of Kerkhoven's ugly contest against Raymond's archrival Clara City:

The game between the Kerkhoven and Clara City teams last Sunday resulted in a victory for the former by a score of 15 to 6. It was an easy game for the Kerkhoven boys after the first inning. Clara City made three runs in the first inning on errors and past balls and led their opponents one, but they did not score again until the latter part of the game. The game was played in a pasture about a mile from town owing to the rain which rendered their town grounds unfit for use. We might also state that the grounds would have been unfit for use under most favorable circumstances and even had it not rained as there was oats on it a foot high and from all appearances the only act done to improve it was the staking of cows on it. It was certainly in fierce condition. However, the pasture where the game was played made a good ground although rather slippery. The Kerkhoven boys played their usually gentlemanly game but this is more than we can say for the other team. They go in to win a game by foul or fair means and started their dirty work in the first inning. The first ball thrown by Bell, the swell-headed poor excuse of a pitcher, nearly crippled the Kerkhoven pitcher [Esten Hanson], striking him right in the small of the back and causing him to drop to the ground. It is generally customary with pitchers when they hit a fellow player to run up and show a feeling of regret, but not so with this swell-head, standing in the box and laughing up his sleeve over the accomplishment of one piece of dirty work. He is either a rotten pitcher or else deliberately throws the ball at the batter for he kept the batters dodging all the time. Another piece of work was when he cried out to the catcher when a man was sliding in home to 'hit him hard.' We might show up some more of his dirty plays in which he did not succeed, such as attempting to trip a base-runner and touching him hard with the ball while running hard to throw him off his feet and possibly incapacitating him from playing any more. There are also others on the team who play equally as dirty ball. J. Keenan gave an exhibition of his skill in intentionally spiking the first baseman, cutting through the shoe leather. This is the way some of the Clara City players treat their visitors after asking them to come down and play a friendly game of ball. It was rank enough to put cannibals to shame to say nothing of ball players who profess to be gentlemen. In justice to those players on the Clara City team who do play clean ball we wish to state that we regret very much that they should be forced to play in such company for there are a number of gentlemanly players on the team. Why even the people of their own town were so disgusted with the treatment given the visitors that they left the grounds saying it was the dirtiest exhibition they had ever witnessed on a diamond. Bro. Archer of The Banner umpired the game and we must say that he favored the Clara City team all through the game, but still they were beefing and kicking on the umpire. The fact of the matter is the team can't play ball fast enough to keep the blood from clogging in their veins and about the only way they could win is with ten men and dirty playing.

The Clara City editor, after admonishing his own team's players for abusive language and careless play, and a number of Raymond citizens for rooting against Clara City, wrote, "Their pitcher is deaf and dumb and while he pitches good ball would not be considered a phenomenon. Our boys got onto him the last two innings but good fielding kept the score down. A deaf and dumb pitcher has one good feature about him and that is no amount of the joshing can rattle him. It would be a good thing sometimes if a whole team was deaf and dumb for then wrangling and jawing at the umpire would cease."

CHAPTER SEVENTEEN

UNHITTABLE ESTEN

Three days later, Benson defeated Kerkhoven 13-12, after Kerkhoven had led 9-0 going into the sixth inning. According to the *Swift County Monitor*, Esten simply ran out of steam after pitching twelve innings over the previous four days. *The Banner* didn't mention any reason, other than the local boys "went to pieces," and Benson enjoyed good fortune, the home crowd, and maybe even a favorable umpire. The Kerkhoven Township correspondent of the *Swift County Monitor* must have been in denial declaring, "All who witnessed the ball game in Benson last Wednesday claim the game in favor of Kerkhoven."

The editor of the *Swift County Monitor* praised Esten, saying, "For five innings did the Benson boys succumb to the curves of Kerkhoven's pitcher, Hanson, not making a run." Benson tallied seven runs in the crucial eighth, and then Kerkhoven catcher

Gordhamer popped up and a Benson fielder doubled the runner off second to end the game. No matter the angle or reason, the defeat tasted bitter.

According to Esten's niece, Verna Johnson Gomer, when Esten disagreed with an umpire's decision, family tradition held that, "he sat down on the mound and wouldn't pitch until the umpire changed his mind." More likely, Esten, the experienced competitor accustomed to bad calls, had a habit of sitting down until an unruly crowd or team stopped arguing with an umpire. John Sundeen, a retired Kerkhoven businessman, recalled from a 1950s conversation with Earl Olson, brother of right fielder Bert Olson, that Esten would squeak in a high, shrill tone when disagreeing with a blown call. Mike Cashman, a former Gallaudet baseball player, said a "squeak" may have been Esten's only means of audibly expressing his frustration.

Given the tension, and unexpected reversal of momentum, Esten may have at times sat down on the mound or squeaked against Benson. It was a devastating loss by any definition. Kerkhoven dropped to 6-1. The squad then had just enough time to try on their new dark green uniforms during a scheduled practice, mentally and emotionally recoup, and figure out how to beat Murdock for the $50 purse at the DeGraff July 4 celebration. The friction among the rivals reached new heights. In his June 19 edition, Archer called the Murdock nine, "10th class players." Continuing the ongoing editorial battle of words with Editor Archer of *The Banner*, *The Murdock Voice*'s editor, E. C. Detuncq, reminded readers on June 25 that his team had narrowly lost to Benson in a razor-tight affair—just as Kerkhoven had lost. Detuncq blasted Archer's writing of the Clara City victory, saying "The Banner must not crow too soon. Pride goeth before a fall."

In late June, Clara City walloped Murdock 7-3.

On July 4 in DeGraff, Minnesota, a thousand people, good food, the Murphy Bros Orchestra, alcoholic beverages—unlike Kerkhoven and Murdock, DeGraff was a wet town—and plenty of wagering all occupied the town. Minnesota School for the Deaf friend Anthony Lykken made the railroad trip in from distant Goodhue County for the holiday rhubarb.

The Banner described the scene:

On account of the rain the program arranged for the forenoon was not carried out. The afternoon sports were, however, carried out as per schedule and were of an interesting character. The best of these was the ball game between the Murdock and Kerkhoven ball clubs. It resulted in a victory for the local team by the very close score of 7 to 8. Both teams put up a very good article of ball although several costly errors were made on both sides. Several exceptionally good plays were made on both sides and up to the time the last Murdock man was out it was by no means certain which team was going to be victorious. Jim Whittemore, of Benson, officiated as umpire in a very satisfactory manner. In fact, his work was so good that he kept the players in both teams in the best of humor and the game was played without any wrangling, played the way a ball game should be played, in an orderly and peaceable manner.

Following are the team lineups and the score by innings:

Kerkhoven	Position	Murdock
Hanson	Pitcher	Casey
O. Gordhamer	Catcher	McCann
H. Johnson	1st b.	Sivertson
J. Johnson	2nd b.	Turnbull
F. L. Johnson	3rd b.	Owens
Mahoney	s. s.	Powers
Olson	r. f.	Olson
Hubbard	l. f.	Duffy
Cox	c. f.	Johnson

Murdock   0 0 2 0 0 0 0 3 2—7
Kerkhoven   0 1 3 1 1 0 2 0 x—8

Game account from the *Murdock Voice*:

It is believed that the least said about the game the better it will be for all concerned. It cannot be said that either team put up the best they could do. However Murdock lost and Kerkhoven has not much to crow over. There was at times several brilliant plays by both sides, the home run by J. J. Johnson in the third, and two double plays, one by Murdock and one by Kerkhoven. But the errors overshadowed the brilliant plays. Two wild throws by Powers and the muff of Cummerford are to a great extent responsible for our defeat. McCann, when struck with the ball by Hanson, was rightfully entitled to first base but the umpire decided otherwise. The Voice is making no excuses, no intimations of fraud, but giving its view of the game as it appeared to the writer on the ground.

Ten days later, basking in victory yet, the Kerkhoven nine took on Benson in a grudge rematch. The previous loss to Benson had been Kerkhoven's only stain. Esten struck out eleven and was virtually unhittable in a lightning fast eighty-minute contest witnessed by 500 rowdy spectators. The Benson squad managed to push across only two runs, losing 4-2. Archer wrote, "Our players bested the Bensonites at handling the willow, but the latter showed up best in fielding and had they been able to decipher Hanson's curves would have stood a very good chance of winning the game."

The Benson Times, the other Benson-based newspaper, reported, "The features of the game were the pitching of Hanson and Thronson, the former striking out 11 men and Thronson giving no bases on balls and fielding his position in fine shape getting seven assists."

After the game, *The Banner* reported on July 17:

A. Westerdahl has resigned as manager of the ball team and Roy Hubbard has been selected in his stead. This is the third manager the boys have had this year, which might cause a disinterested outsider to conclude that the boys are a trifle hard to manage. However that may be, they have demonstrated that they know how to play ball, having lost but one game so far this season, and have the united and hearty support of all our people. It wouldn't be a bad idea, though, if the boys would make up their minds that managers are elected to 'manage' and read up on that portion of the holy writ which tells of what happens to a house that is divided against itself.

Trying to increase its fame while still possessing the means, the Kerkhoven team decided on tackling a tough all-star team from

Willmar in the neutral town of Spicer. Another fundraiser brought in a sufficient amount to cover rail tickets, which were seventy-five cents round trip. The hungry Willmar All Stars were chomping at the bit. They had vanquished Kandiyohi 25-8 only a week earlier. It was David versus Goliath. The city of Kerkhoven had 411 citizens, Willmar, about 3,400.

The Spicer correspondent to Willmar's *The Republican Gazette*, wrote this lengthy, biblical-type report of the game—his target being a former Kerkhoven resident, now residing on the shores of Green Lake at Spicer:

Clad in a cap of snowy white, commonly supposed by superstitious people to be the emblem of purity, Judas Iscariot II stood on the Spicer baseball field last Sunday in the guise of an umpire and according to his decisions the victors became the vanquished. It was the living over again of the man who for a few pieces of silver was willing to betray the confidence of his superiors in the beginning of the twentieth century just as the man with the dark face and sinister look did in certain other days away back at a time when a man's life was at par with a man's honor. Act I, Scene I.

The second act, with scene 2 opened on the hill of skulls on the west side, otherwise known as the Spicer Athletic Park, shortly after noon last Sunday and a large crowd was present to witness a promised game of baseball. Nobody expected to see a highway robbery and this is where the surprise came in. For five innings one side bravely fought the opponents and the umpire and all other visible or invisible evil influences while the other had all hands heaving to keep up their course. It was the Willmar 'All Stars' against the Kerkhoven club, and Spicer was about evenly divided in bestowing its sentiments and rootings when the game began. After it was finished the crowd was unanimous in their opinion that the 'All Stars' had been robbed of victory rightfully theirs, by the reincarnated Judas.

The second act opened with the reincarnated Judas strolling into the diamond with a big, black cigar in his face. Ludvig Glarum stood on the slab for the visitors and threw nothing but what an honest man might have hit with a shovel. For five innings he threw these slants and they proved even too beguiling for the boys from up the line.

The third scene pictured the R. J. prostrate on the sand. For five innings he had persisted in declaring all of the suffering Glarum's slants vile brands and thereby breathed the breath of life into the emaciated nostrils of the opposing horses. Several scores had been acquired in this way by the Kerkhoven boys but no protest had been raised by the 'All Stars.'

Only one score separated the two teams but it was painfully evident that Mr. Glarum had hold of the wrong end. Accordingly, when the R. J. gave his decision on what should have been three strikes, the meek and patient Glarum put a bug on him and there was an 'Empire' razed to the sands. After that matters got steadily worse and the breach became impassable until finally the agony ended with the reincarnated Judas nailing the 'All Stars' to the crucifixion tree with a margin of two suffering, sweating, kidnapped scores.

The last act closed with the tableau of 10 to 8 and the umpire is said to have won a handsome wager over the result. After that he kept scarce, but the Kerkhoven boys, who were all gentlemen, did not deem the laurels righteously won for the honors due the vanquished will not fit their wear. Being gentlemen they do not glory over the victory that is not righteously theirs. Of the game in its entirety there is not much to say, looking at it from an impartial standpoint. Both teams played an excellent game and the score would have been much smaller with honest umpiring. As it was many a promising base runner was murdered on the first sack or at the home plate or in base running by notoriously rotten decisions. The Kerkhoven boys have a strong team and a very steady pitcher. Their field work was fine, but at the bat they need to develop more strength. The 'All Stars' were far superior as far as all around ball playing goes and satisfied the crowd of spectators to that effect. In relative size the Kerkhoven boys are much heavier. They throw with greater force, but in the harmonious team work the 'All Stars' are superior.

Hugh Campbell, for the 'All Stars,' made a home run. Many good catches stand to their credit. At a future date we are promised another game and we hope the objectionable spectacle of having an umpire rob the boys in broad daylight will be eliminated. The spectacle is disgusting in the extreme and does not recommend even a young man who has money up on the game.

The Banner's story reads as follows:

The Kerkhoven ball club went to Spicer and the following day played a game with the Willmar team on the Spicer grounds. Our boys won by a score of 8 to 10. Victor Hultgren, of Green Lake, umpired the game and it seems did not give entire satisfaction as the Willmar pitcher attempted to lick him. Cooler heads prevented a row, however, and the game was concluded. The boys say the Spicer ball ground is very poor, being located on the side of a hill, and are of the opinion that had the game been played on their own or some other good grounds the score would have been much lower. Quite a number of our people went over to witness the game.

A week later after reading *The Republican Gazette*, Editor Archer replied with both barrels:

The Spicer correspondent to the Willmar Republican Gazette made an uncalled for and libelous attack on the young man who umpired the ball game played at Spicer two weeks ago between the Willmar and Kerkhoven ball clubs. The article in question appeared in last week's issue of the *Gazette* and those of our people who witnessed the game are unanimous in pronouncing it wholly untrue, and say that in their opinion the umpire gave the Willmar aggregation a shade the best of it. Our ball team does not have to be favored by the umpire in order to win from any aggregation of ball players in this part of the state and if the Willmar 'All Stars' are not yet convinced of that fact they should come up here some afternoon, where there is a good ground to play on, and have another game with the boys. If they do we'll guarantee that the 'R' column on their score card will show enough goose eggs to make about three sittings of three.

Esten remembered Dassel from 1902 at Eden Valley, and his two close defeats. Nothing changed. Kerkhoven fell to Dassel 6-3, their first home defeat of the year, and the team's season record stood at 9-2. Dassel won the contest by stealing thirteen bases against catcher Gordhamer, who was credited with four passed balls. Esten hit eighth in the line-up and went hitless in four at bats, struck out sixteen, and walked only one. Editor Archer couldn't resist one parting shot, "A large delegation from Murdock was down to see the game. Among the number were several of those long-eared, feeble-minded brayers who think it an evidence of intelligence to criticize the decisions of the party who umpired the game."

The rematch, played in Dassel, received an emotional build-up from the *Dassel Anchor* editor: "Kerkhoven will play in Dassel next Sunday at 3:00 p.m. They have a mute pitcher who has speed and curves to burn. The game will be a warm one from start to finish." For some reason, the competitive teams located about fifty miles apart called off the game.

In late August, the *Murdock Voice* editor was still smarting from his team's July 4 spanking at the hands of archrival Kerkhoven, and his rage finally boiled over while commenting on Editor Archer and *The Banner*:

The above from the Kerkhoven Banner deserves to be annexed to such papers as the Arizona Kicker, Police Gazette and others of that ilk. Our people who went to Kerkhoven to witness a good game of ball, and after paying an admission fee of 25 cents to be thus insulted and maligned by one who ought to have been thankful that the gate receipts had been augmented to a sufficiency to pay the expenses incurred, is simply adding insult to injury, and should not be countenanced by any respectable people.

Let us hope that the majority of the Kerkhoven people will condemn the utterances of one whose thinking apparatus is out of gear. It comes with poor grace after the kind treatment the people of our neighboring village have received from our people whenever they have visited us, to be maligned and held to scorn and ridicule by one who ought to have known better. The privileges of the public at a ball game should not be abridged, as one of the prerogatives is to roast the umpire.

Make no wrong decisions.

Be impartial!

By so doing you will not be writing or printing such insulting items as the one quoted above.

Well, you've got to hope again. A majority of the Kerkhoven people do not condemn the utterance. On the contrary they feel that it was a deserved criticism and only complain that it was not strong enough.

When did the Kerkhoven people receive kind treatment at the hands of Murdock people? We hadn't heard about that. A few weeks ago a number of our people went up there to witness the Benson-Murdock ball game and the 'kind treatment' they received that day was to be compelled to stay out in a heavy rain storm. The Murdock people were not even hospitable enough to open their doors and give them shelter when they rapped for admittance.

The Dassel rematch happened, despite Kerkhoven being short-handed because of Johnny and Frank Johnson having to visit relatives in Minneapolis. Manager Hubbard contracted three Appleton players as last-minute substitutes. The *Dassel Anchor* described the rematch:

>It was a very weird exhibition of ball playing that the local ball team put up last Sunday against the team from Kerkhoven—that is, part of it was. Our boys failed to put up anything that looked like an attempt to play ball and errors were as numerous and costly as flies in the good old summer time. It was certainly an off day and that is about the most charitable view that can be taken of the game. The Kerkhoven team played but little better and had our boys batted in their usual form the score might have been a little more even at least. The visitors were padded considerably with three basemen from the fast Appleton team and the kicking of these players was another disagreeable feature to accompany the ragged playing.

Kerkhoven feasted off Dassel pitching and won going away 15-4 as Esten struck out eleven. *The Banner* added: "Hanson pitched his usual good game, his curves proving a puzzle to the Dassel players." In the stands, rooting for Kerkhoven at Dassel, was friend Lue Evenson.

The following game featured Kerkhoven besting the Willmar All Stars at Kerkhoven. They played what many believed was their best baseball of the long season, winning 4-3, and turning three double plays. The newspaper recognized Esten for his "benders" and thirteen strike-outs, and the outing could have been a personal high-water mark. Of course, a spirited delegation from Murdock obnoxiously hooted for Willmar. Kerkhoven finished the 1903 season at 11-2. Various newspapers reported pitcher strike-out totals in only five games, and in those, Esten averaged about thirteen per game.

Esten succeeded at pitching, but he wouldn't be anyone or anywhere without his catchers, particularly Happy Gordhamer, who literally gave up his body to catch Esten. The author, early in life, saw firsthand Happy's fingers, which were bent and twisted from catching in an era that lacked modern-day protective garb. In a 2004 personal interview, Happy's son, Bob, told of his father's broken fingers that never healed, because of dozens of errant foul tips and wild pitches catching Happy's exposed fingers.

1903 BASE BALL SCHEDULE
KERKHOVEN, MINN.

DATE	OPPONENT	PLAYED AT	WINNER
May 17	Murdock	Murdock	Kerkhoven, 17-12
May 30	Murdock	Kerkhoven	Kerkhoven, 16-9
June 17	Louriston-Smith	Kerkhoven	Kerkhoven, 19-2
June 14	Raymond	Kerkhoven	Kerkhoven, 19-7
June 20	Raymond	Raymond	Kerkhoven, 13-10
June 21	Clara City	Clara City	Kerkhoven, 15-6
June 24	Benson	Benson	Benson, 13-12
July 4	Murdock	DeGraff	Kerkhoven, 8-7
July 10	Benson	Kerkhoven	Kerkhoven, 4-2
July 19	Willmar "All Stars"	Kerkhoven	Kerkhoven, 10-8
August 9	Dassel	Kerkhoven	Dassel, 6-3
August 23	Dassel	Dassel	Kerkhoven, 15-4
August 30	Willmar "All Stars"	Kerkhoven	Kerkhoven, 4-3

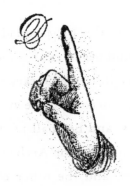

CHAPTER EIGHTEEN

BOSTON BLOOMERS

While Esten was becoming a Minnesota amateur baseball legend, the Wright brothers boldly believed they could fly in a machine. They did in December 1903 at Kitty Hawk, North Carolina. Closer to home, another bold invention revealed that year was the horseless carriage, first brought to Kerkhoven by L. Nyquist, who purchased a six-horsepower Rambler and drove it in from Minneapolis. By all accounts, Esten was changing local perceptions of what a deaf man could accomplish. Many people believed he was the best amateur pitcher in western Minnesota.

Among other amazing changes wafting across Minnesota that winter was the startling decision by editors of the *Murdock Voice*, *Kerkhoven Banner*, *Appleton Press and Tribune*, and both Benson papers to create an editors and publishers association, to reduce angry rhetoric, and to work for common good.

Hungry for more glory, the 1904 squad organized in early January, elected officers, and began raising money, at first $52.25 by selling "leap year baskets" during a literary and musical program held on January 29. Players decorated the village's town hall with dark green uniforms, bats, and baseball paraphernalia. Not bad for the dead of winter, wrote Editor Archer. The new manager elected was R. W. Hamon, and the other officers elected were Raymond Cox, secretary; and Henry Johnson, treasurer. In early March, hired-gun shortstop Henry Mahoney returned from Alexandria, Minnesota, for another summer of baseball, and ten days later the team held another fund-raising event. The baseball boys sponsored an entertainment and dance in the town hall on Friday, March 18. During the agonizing wait for spring, Kerkhoven players whittled away their winter blues at the town's new bowling alley, which player Henry Johnson had recently co-purchased with his brother-in-law Marcus Irgens.

The *Swift County Review*, based in Benson, wrote, "Kerkhoven has already commenced gathering together ball players and as far as possible are employing players of known abilities as a requisite qualification. If possible Kerkhoven proposes to have the club of this section this year." The Clara City and Raymond newspapers mentioned Kerkhoven offering players summer employment and "flattering inducements."

The ball club organized a third fund-raising event—another basket social on April 8—ladies being requested to bring baskets and gentlemen to bring well-filled purses. The first exhibition game occurred in near-winter conditions in late April, when the Kerkhoven "regulars" and manager Bob Hamon hammered an unidentified Kerkhoven "All-Star" team 11-4 at home over five innings. The return match happened on May 6 with the "regulars" again prevailing 11-0.

The May 6 edition of *The Banner* noted recent baseball rule changes, including this dandy: "A trick play that heretofore was not covered by any rule will this season result disastrously to the perpetrator. Should a coacher at third base start for the plate to draw a play from a fielder the runner entitled to that will be declared out for such interference. Two coaches instead of one as formerly will be allowed."

Esten Hanson was absent thus far in the season. Mahoney pitched in his place, and perhaps Ray Cox.

In mid-May, *The Banner* settled the mystery: "Esten Hanson returned from Otter Tail County last week. He came here on Wednesday and contracted with manager Hamon to pitch for the ball team again this year. He will now remain in town all the time during the ball season. Mr. Hamon is to be congratulated on securing Mr. Hanson again this year as he is undoubtedly one of the best pitchers in the state and is already in excellent shape for the summer's work." Kerkhoven won the final exhibition game over the All Stars 3-2, Mahoney pitching, and the official season began.

On May 15, Kerkhoven battled Morris, considered one of the state's better amateur teams, before 500 raucous Kerkhoven spectators. Morris traveled via rail and brought its rooters and the Morris Military Band, which played. Kerkhoven quieted their drums and bugles by winning 11-3, with Esten fanning sixteen batters and hurling a shutout into the eighth inning. Now living in town and not forced to pedal eleven miles in for each game, Esten had a great deal more stamina, and it showed. Curious players from Benson, DeGraff, Murdock, Pennock, and Willmar also attended the game, no doubt scouting the loaded Kerkhoven nine.

On May 19, the *Morris Sun* reported the score as a more appealing 10-5, and attributed the loss to their not having their best players on hand. Two days later, another town newspaper, *The Morris Tribune*, merely noted of the rematch that, "Mayor Hause has given the baseball boys to understand that the police will have instructions to stop the game. The mayor's action will meet with almost unanimous approval. Everyone has the right to spend the Sabbath as he may see fit, as long as he does not interfere with someone else doing the same. The Sunday ball game, especially in a small town, interferes too much with the rights of people to spend Sunday that way."

In effect, the mayor's printed threat caused the Kerkhoven team to cancel, for fear their hard-earned money would be wasted on fruitless travel. Still itching to play, the team hurriedly scheduled another game for the same day against Raymond, and Kerkhoven and Esten smothered their offense like a wet blanket, 3-0. So far, in eighteen innings of baseball against very good competition, Esten had yielded only three runs.

On May 27, the editor of the Raymond News wrote in part:

"However they were justly entitled to one run. With a man on third Hanson made a bock [sic] and the base runner was entitled to a base, which would have brought in a score, but as the new bock rule had not been enforced very strictly prior to this play it was overlooked. Mat Thom acted in the capacity of umpire and although some of his decisions brought forth criticism on both sides, he tried to be fair and impartial, as anyone will testify to who witnessed the game. The Kerkhoven boys speak very highly of the treatment they received here and are anxious for the opportunity to reciprocate when our boys play the return game."

On the road, May 30, and against an Atwater club carrying pitcher Tom Riffe, formerly of the Dassel squad that had given Esten Hanson so many fits, Kerkhoven lost 4-3 in eleven innings. *The Banner* commented: "It was certainly a good exhibition of the national sport, as good a game of ball as one could wish to see. It was, in the main, a pitcher's battle, the hits made by both nines being few and far between."

The Boston Bloomers, a female baseball team, had toured through western Minnesota in 1899. The Bloomers had crushed the egos of Benson 12-6 before a couple of hundred curious spectators while employing two male players and the astonishing pitching of Maude Nelson. The ladies played mostly in larger towns that could produce substantial gate receipts. The Ladies Vintage Baseball Association website on January 1, 2003, remarked,

> Toward the end of the [nineteenth] century, many barnstorming ladies 'bloomer' clubs formed. These clubs usually had typically one to three male players and would play against men's clubs. Perhaps the most successful female player and ultimately team was Maude Nelson. Born in Italy in 1881 to the name Clementina Brida, Nelson became the premier female pitcher of the later 19th and early 20th century. She played on the Boston Bloomers before joining forces with her husband, John Olson, owner of the Cherokee Indian baseball Club in 1908.

The National Italian American Sports Hall of Fame website reported, "She learned to play baseball when she was a child and took the name 'Maude Nelson.' Before she was 16, she was pitching for the Boston Bloomer Girls, who traveled across the country in 1897. She started virtually every day, though she often pitched only a few innings and then moved to third base for the rest of the game."

In early June, *The Banner* reported:

Our baseball team will play an exhibition game with the Boston Bloomers on Thursday, June 9, at 3 o'clock. The Bloomer Girls do not expect to draw crowds entirely on account of the novelty of being lady baseball players, but really put up a very creditable exhibition of the national game. They travel in a private palace car and carry a canvas fence 14 feet high and 1,200 feet long for enclosing the grounds, a canopy covered grand stand with a capacity of 2,000, and everything necessary to give a first-class exhibition. They have toured every state, also Canada, and have everywhere received good notices from the press, not only for their good baseball playing but also for their ladylike behavior.

Further, the Boston Bloomers promoted themselves as the "Ladies' Champion Base Ball Club of the World." After playing Kerkhoven, the team would take on Atwater the next day. Before the lady Bloomers, and Maude Nelson's fastball, though, Kerkhoven had an all-important game against pesky Atwater, which had pummeled Kerkhoven pride only weeks before. This time Kerkhoven conquered 4-2, with opposing hurlers Riffe and Hanson each having ten strikeouts in another hot pitching duel.

With the Bloomers game occurring right before the press deadline, Editor Archer was only able to write one paragraph. Esten didn't pitch because of having to toss a full nine innings only two days prior. No way would manager Bob Hamon tire his star pitcher with another important contest occurring in three short days. Yet eight hundred people filled the specially made stands to take in the circus-like spectacle, which the women easily won, 19-8. On the next day, the Bloomers and Atwater tied 6-6 before the Bloomers had to leave on the noon train. For many people in Kerkhoven, that day was one of the most exciting in their town history.

The Kerkhoven loss to a women's team seemed to amuse *Murdock Voice*'s E. C. Detuncq, who suddenly forgot his winter vow to bury the hatchet. He chided the Kerkhoven team for being "too big for their britches."

Editor Archer replied:

Just why some of the people in our little sister village, Murdock, should feel sore because Kerkhoven has a good ball team is more than we can understand. In last week's issue of the *Voice* the editor of that faded sheet gives vent to that sore feeling in a write-up of the ball game our boys played with the Boston Bloomers. That our boys were defeated was undoubtedly the cause of much rejoicing up that way and some of the 'sore ones' forthwith called on the *Voice* man and gave him to understand that he must 'roast' the boys, and that 'easy mark,' ever willing to do another's bidding, proceeded to do as he was told. The 'roast,' though, was a rather far-fetched affair and will in no wise affect the reputation of the organization assailed, the best amateur team in western Minnesota.

Detuncq smelled blood:

The young man who edits the paper down the line is

seriously affected over our report and comments of the Bloomers-Kerkhoven ball game. It is to be regretted that some people are so thick headed that they cannot see a joke. We always supposed that a newspaper had a right to make comments on any and all happenings, but the *Banner* man says no! Why? Because when the Kerkhoven team is defeated that must not be proclaimed outside of that village, but when they win, that must be shouted from the house tops, that Kerkhoven has won another game. And again, no newspaper must print anything only what will be commendatory of the people of that village. Should the people tell the *Banner* man not to print a certain article, does he respect the wishes of his supporters? Of course he does! Why should he condemn in others that which he himself does? 'Jaded Sheet.' Will someone explain that riddle, if it be one? Let it be understood, that THE VOICE will continue to publish the news, whether it be a ball game, a dogfight or any other happening which may be of interest to our readers. We have always tried to be fair in our dealing with the Kerkhoven baseball team. When they won a game we gave them credit. And when they lost one the people knew it. Last year the Murdock ball team lost several games. Did we keep still? No! Our files show that we commented rather severely, pointing out the deficiency of some of the players which caused them to play better ball afterwards. People who live in glass houses should not throw stones.

The newspaper editor truce in Swift County had lasted exactly six months.

Kerkhoven fans traveled down the line to Spicer for another David versus Goliath match-up against the young-buck Willmar All Stars, except star Esten was not able to pitch. Manager Bob Hamon, in a pinch, had to hire Riffe, the Atwater and Dassel very talented pitcher, and he shutout Willmar 2-0, while striking out eleven and walking four.

The Banner filled in the blanks: "Hanson, the regular Kerkhoven pitcher, was not in shape to pitch the game and Riffe, of the Atwater club, was secured to take his place. At the game played here on Thursday (against the Bloomers) of last week, Hanson and B. Olson ran into each other, while trying to catch a fly ball, and both were quite badly hurt. Hanson's nose was dislocated and his chest and side were quite sore for several days. Olson was also quite badly disfigured and his usual handsome countenance has not presented a very attractive appearance since, as one eye is very, very black."

While playing center field, Esten had collided with right fielder Bertie Olson. Certainly, he wouldn't have been able to hear Bertie Olson call for the ball, and Esten may not have been able to effectively call off Olson. On June 16 and still hurting from the Boston Bloomers game, Esten nonetheless had an excellent pitching effort in a 3-1 loss to Morris, striking out nine. The Morris newspaper indirectly praised Esten, saying, "Stewart's [Morris player] all around playing was perhaps the feature of the game. He had three hard fielding chances to his credit, and batted like veteran, securing three hits out of three turns at bat. When he left the 'field of battle,' he had a batting percentage of 1.000, which may be considered a remarkable record against any pitcher, but especially so against such a man as the one who pitched for Kerkhoven."

A third game with Morris would give Kerkhoven winter bragging rights, and regain a modicum of pride, and it did, as they won 5-3, at home, in front of 200 fans. Esten struck out nine, walked one, and carried a shutout into the seventh inning. *The Morris Sun* reported, in part, "Morris was unable to connect with the obliquities [curve balls] of the deaf and dumb pitcher, and only made four hits, while Bailey, our boasted southpaw, held his opponents down to seven." Batting sixth, behind slugger Mahoney, Esten had two hits and a run batted in.

Kerkhoven ran its record to 11-2, after beating New Paynesville, 10-1, and the Willmar All Stars, 6-5, both games in Spicer. In the first game, the *Wilmar Tribune* reported that Esten was throwing "crooked twisters" while striking out twelve in a one-hitter. The newspaper continued, "[Kerkhoven has] an excellent pitcher and [they] give him good support. The team is one of which both Manager Hamon and the citizens of Kerkhoven have good reasons to be proud."

CHAPTER NINETEEN

$65 PITCHER

The July I contest at home against Benson featured a highly disputed call. In the bottom of the ninth, with two outs, and after having scored two runs that inning, Kerkhoven had the momentum with runners on second and third. The runner on third took a long lead, and when the Benson pitcher tried picking him off, the Kerhoven runner broke for home. In the ensuing collision, the catcher dropped the ball, and the umpire called the runner out despite numerous Kerkhoven protests. Benson won, 3-2. Editor Archer blamed the blown call on "a number of spectators and players" crowding around home base, obstructing the umpire's view.

The *Swift County Monitor* uncharacteristically gave an exhaustive blow-by-blow account of the game, and in the process, revealed Esten's monthly wage: "Kerkhoven's $65 pitcher proved to be an easy mark for our boys, and Riffe, a borrowed pitcher from Atwater, was duly installed into the box in the sixth inning." Immediately after pitching for Kerkhoven in that game, Riffe contracted with Graceville for $75 per month, plus expenses. He would never again wear the dark green uniform of Kerkhoven.

After reading the *Swift County Monitor*'s write-up, which included not-so-kind descriptions of Kerkhoven players, Editor Archer took aim:

> In writing up the Benson-Kerkhoven ball game of two weeks ago, a reporter for the *Swift County Monitor* intimates that our boys are not to be considered as being in the same class as the Benson team. Just why that small caliber individual should have any such fool notions as that we don't know, and care less, but we have been authorized to state that if he, or any of his cohorts, have faith in that assertion they will be given an opportunity to corner a whole lot of good Kerkhoven money if the Benson ball team can make good. Kerkhoven people stand willing to back their team for any amount of money Benson people may name if another game can be arranged for between the two teams.

The daring challenge piqued Benson interest.

On July 4 in Spicer, Kerkhoven took out Atwater, 6-3, even though Esten, Roy Hubbard, Ray Cox, and Oliver Hubbard missed the game because of a train wreck up the line near Morris. Kerkhoven recruited four able-bodied players on hand, and Mahoney struck out twelve, in front of 1,000 spectators.

Kerkhoven was on a roll. The team beat DeGraff at home 4-1 in front of 500 fans. The next day, and playing in New Paynesville, Esten faced his former ball club, Eden Valley, and posted a heady 1-0 win. Winning that game must have felt awfully good.

With Esten absent from the mound the following day against New Paynesville, Kerkhoven lost 9-1—only a couple of weeks earlier, Kerkhoven had beaten them, 10-1.

Bob Hamon's 1904 crew had not gone unnoticed in Minnesota amateur baseball circles. Editor Archer in *The Banner* quoted the manager: "He is now of the opinion that his aggregation is swift enough for the fastest company 'what is.'"

Also in the June 10 issue, the editor wrote: "Kerkhoven is certainly getting an enviable reputation as a base-ball town. Yesterday the manager of the Renville team which is reputed to be the best amateur team in the state, phoned Manager Hamon asking if our boys could come over there on Tuesday of next week for a game. Owing to the fact that the boys are to play two games with the Willmar team between now and then, Mr. Hamon concluded that his men would not likely be in the best of shape at that time so declined the game but assures us that he will arrange for a couple of games with the Renville team before the season is over. Pretty fast company, but we believe our lads will be able to hold 'em down."

Renville wasn't about to be put off by a team that may have represented a threat to their reputation. To prove superiority, the Renville manager agreed to travel to Kerkhoven for the game—if they received a guarantee of part of the gate receipts.

Hamon, knowing that his boys would relish testing their base-ball skills against the Renvillites, especially their famous black pitcher, agreed to the proposal, scheduling the game for Saturday, July 16.

The Banner excitedly announced on July 15: "No doubt the best ball game of the season will be that to be played here tomorrow (Saturday) afternoon between the Renville and Kerkhoven teams.

Holland [William "Billy"], the renowned colored pitcher, will be in the box for the visitors. 'Twill be worth the price of admission to see him twirl the ball. The members of the home team are working themselves into fine form for the game and a battle royal is a certainty. Game will be called at 3:00 o'clock sharp. You can't afford to miss seeing it."

Swinging for the Fences, edited by Steven R. Hoffbeck, commented on the effect of black players in Minnesota baseball in the early 1900s: "They [St. Cloud] hoped that Ball would help them to compete with the Waseca team, the prior year's state champion, which was led by black pitchers George Wilson and William (Billy) Holland." And, "The Waseca EACO Flour team had been one of the best in Minnesota in 1900 and 1901 due to the one-two pitching duo of George Wilson and Billy Holland, veteran pitchers who had played for the great Chicago area black teams in the late 1890s."

Also noted by Hoffbeck was the effect players such as Billy Holland may have had on gate receipts: "... [a] black ball player was a real curiosity in many parts of the state. The novelty factor involved in having a black player had the tendency to increase attendance...."

Esten, locked in a pitcher's duel two days earlier, came away with a 1-0 win. Recognizing Esten's arm wouldn't be revived with only a one-day rest, Manager Hamon brought in Booth, a known quantity, as his pitcher.

Editor Archer, perhaps sensing the uniqueness of the July 16 game, wrote on July 22:

> Saturday afternoon the boys were again defeated, this time by the fast Renville team. The score for this game was 8 to 1. The one score our boys got was made in the ninth inning after everyone had concluded they were going to

draw a shut-out. The Renville team is a very swift Aggregation of ball players and considering that our boys were somewhat tired out and sore as a result of having played the two previous days the showing they made against so fast a team was not bad. Only a small crowd, mostly town people, was out to see the game. Our boys had guaranteed the Renville team $50. The gate receipts fell $15 short of that amount.

Holland, the famous negro pitcher, was in the box for the visitors and fully satisfied the crowd that he is entitled to the fame he has attained as a twirler. Booth, of Willmar, pitched the first five innings for the Kerkhoven team and his delivery was touched up for seven of the eight runs made by the visitors. Hanson pitched the last four innings, and held the heavy hitting Renvilleites down to a few scratch hits, only one run being made after he was put in the box.

Editor Archer, the team, and the fans (after two years experience) may have come to realize how many dollars were necessary to support a better than average ball club. While the Boston Bloomers game attracted 800 fans, the Renville game drew a small crowd of "mostly town people"—conspicuously absent were baseball fans from nearby towns and farms. Archer may have purposely illustrated what was involved if a village wanted to field a championship team, when on September 16, and without comment, he published a summary of Renville's 1904 season: "'The baseball season for the Renville team closed last Saturday with the game at Bird Island. The team has been a success both as to the work performed and the advertising it gave the town, and we understand another team will be sent out from here next year, and whatever mistakes were made this year will be remedied next season. With the single exception of Chippewa Falls, who came ahead in the final wind up, and breaking even with Webster, the team came home a winner over all the other teams they met. They played 82 games and won 55 of them.' (*Renville Star Farmer*)."

1904 BASE BALL SCHEDULE
KERKHOVEN "Regular" TEAM
KERKHOVEN, MINN.

DATE	OPPONENT	PLAYED AT	WINNER
April 24	Kerk. All Stars	Kerkhoven	Kerkhoven, 11-4
May 1	Kerk. All Stars	Kerkhoven	Kerkhoven, 11-0
May 8	Kerk. All Stars	Kerkhoven	Kerkhoven, 3-2
May 15	Morris	Kerkhoven	Kerkhoven, 11-3
May 22	Raymond	Raymond	Kerkhoven, 4-0
May 30	Atwater	Atwater	Atwater, 4-3
June 7	Atwater	Kerkhoven	Kerkhoven, 4-2
June 9	Boston Bloomers	Kerkhoven	B. Bloomers, 19-8
June 12	Willmar "All Stars"	Spicer	Kerkhoven, 2-0
June 16	Morris	Morris	Morris, 3-1
June 21	Morris	Kerkhoven	Kerkhoven, 5-3
June 24	New Paynesville	Spicer	Kerkhoven, 10-1
June 26	Willmar "All Stars"	Spicer	Kerkhoven, 6-5
June 29	Benson	Benson (3 inns.)	Benson, 4-2 (rain)
July 1	Benson	Kerkhoven	Benson, 3-2
July 4	Atwater	Spicer	Kerkhoven, 6-3
July 10	DeGrafff	Kerkhoven	Kerkhoven, 4-1
July 14	Eden Valley	New Paynesville	Kerkhoven, 1-0
July 15	New Paynesville	New Paynesville	N. Paynesville, 9-1
July 16	Renville	Kerkhoven	Renville, 8-1

CHAPTER TWENTY

BATTLE LAKE AND ON

An April 1905 editorial may have sealed Esten's baseball fate for the upcoming season. Editor Archer wrote in *The Banner*:

There is talk of organizing a ball team here for the coming summer. In past years the ball teams we have had attained a state-wide reputation as one of the best amateur clubs in the state and we can see no reasons why a team cannot be organized again this year that will fully sustain that reputation. We believe this can and should be done without importing a single player. A team composed of all home players could be run cheaper and would be even more loyally supported by the people of the village than an aggregation made up in part of hired men. It's time to move in the matter and if someone will start the ball rolling we believe sufficient funds can be secured from the local business men to defray the expenses of maintaining a team. Get busy boys, so there will be something doing to create a little excitement during the quiet summer months.

Three weeks later, a baseball club organized with these players: Bert Olson, Raymond Cox, Bert Hennessy, Arthur Johnson, George Thonvold, Ford Pritchard, Henry Johnson, Oliver Gordhamer, George Gordhamer, and Johnny Johnson. The team named its new managers: thirty-year-old Archer and the town barber, Wood. Hanson, Riffe, Booth, Turner, Mahoney, McCann, and Manager Bob Hamon were not on this new team. Apparently, the financial burden of fielding a cutting-edge team had proved too much. Within a month, sadly, the depleted Kerkhoven squad disbanded after only a handful of games, the last being when Raymond angrily walked off the field in protest. For young men grown accustomed to being the best, average no longer held attraction.

Visitors often described Battle Lake as being beautiful, pressed against the western shore of West Battle Lake in Otter Tail County, near Fergus Falls, deep in the heart of a major lake district about eighty-five miles northwest of Sunburg. Battle Lake had plenty of good fishing, hunting, and trapping. When learning of being rejected by the Kerkhoven club, Esten wasted no time beelining for Otter Tail County, where his aunt, uncle, and three younger male cousins lived, in rural Vining.

In late April, the *Battle Lake Review* picked up the story: "Esten Hanson of Vining was in Battle Lake Monday to look up the chance for securing a position in the ball team which it is proposed to organize. Mr. Hanson is deaf and dumb and attended the Faribault school for the deaf for seven years. He worked in the printing department at the school."

Esten had left home after Easter, and upon arrival in Battle Lake, immediately contacted the local newspaper editor. Esten, after all, besides being a baseballist, was a trained printer, and could have been looking for work. One of his cousins may have helped communicate his passion of playing baseball to the editor. It was highly unlikely that anyone in Battle Lake, which wasn't much larger than Kerkhoven, understood sign language. Within a week, the Battle Lake squad called a practice game, in part to test "the skill of the deaf mute pitcher," the editor wrote, "... [who] appeared clever and will probably play with the local team this season. A deaf ball player wouldn't become rattled through any effort of the rooters."

The Fergus Falls newspaper in mid-May reported Esten as being "Battle Lake's pitcher." He further enhanced his reputation by pitching for the Vining squad on Syttende Mai, May 17, Norway's major holiday.

Esten, a mature twenty-seven years old, and the Battle Lake Lakers beat the Wadena nine by a 7–5 score on May 21. The *Battle Lake Review* reported, "The game was warmly contested from the time the first ball flew over the plate until the last echo of the rooters' voices died away. There was both clever and bad playing, but the game was an interesting one, and much attention was centered on Hanson, the deaf mute who pitched part of the game for Battle Lake. He played with the nine at the Faribault school for the deaf for a number of years and is a clever player; but no one ever heard him say a word about it."

Next, in Battle Lake, the Breckenridge team bested an all-star contingent that included some Battle Lake players, 5–4. The Breckenridge pitcher, Thatcher, had, at one time, pitched for the University of Wisconsin. The *Wilkin County Gazette* (Breckenridge) and *Fergus Falls Weekly Journal* did not record Esten as participating. The Breckenridge hero was their team captain, Thomas, who blasted a two-run shot in the ninth.

The June 16–18 weekend in Battle Lake featured a Modern Woodmen of America picnic, speeches, lively dances to organ music, and a baseball tournament. It was unseasonably cold. Rain showers canceled the Friday game, but on Saturday and Sunday Battle Lake swept three, one from Clitheral, 7-2, and a pair from Wadena, 4-3 and 3-0. From newspaper accounts, Esten shared pitching duties with hurlers Lund and Ogsbury. The next weekend, Battle Lake beat Vining 7-0, a game Esten probably pitched in because of Vining being his relatives' hometown. In the second game, Staples squeezed past Battle Lake 4-3, in part due to Battle Lake missing its star catcher and slugger, the injured Anton Jenson.

After sweeping a pair from Clitherall, and earning a $50 purse, the Battle Lake nine scheduled a rematch with Breckenridge. The *Fergus Falls Weekly Journal* described the game: "The fast Battle Lake baseball team went to Breckenridge Sunday and was defeated 6 to 2. The Battle Lake boys do not take kindly to their defeat, however, for the umpire deliberately robbed them of the game. His decisions were so unfair that even the Breckenridge fans were disgusted. Arrangements are now under way to lay Breckenridge two games, one at Fergus Falls and the other at Battle Lake, and the Battle Lake boys hope to win both games, provided a fair and impartial umpire is secured."

The *Battle Lake Review* seconded:

Battle Lake lost to Breckenridge Sunday—not because Breckenridge played better ball, but on account of a certain individual who stands behind the pitcher's box and who is generally called the umpire. What title to give this party is hard to decide, but his decisions for Battle Lake were worse that the odor which arises from a broken egg which has lain for a month in a warm place. We will not mention his name out of respect to his friends. The score was 6 to 2 and would have been much worse if Breckenridge could possibly have had more men to get to bases, once on first it meant a score, for the umpire seemed to lose his sense of sight when Breckenridge players were out, and would always call them safe. Battle Lake on three separate occasions had crowded bases and chances to win the game, but about this time his majesty would hand out rotten decisions like a hog digging up vegetables in a garden, and Battle Lake's hopes of winning would be smaller than ever. Hanson pitched the first four innings and Lund finished the game. Lund was steadier than Hansen [sic], only allowing one score in five innings. It is always hard to lose a game, but doubly more so when the umpire is the cause. Breckenridge comes to Battle Lake soon, and the boys here will at least have a fair umpire.

The columnist for the *Breckenridge Gazette*, of course, saw the game from a completely different angle: "A good crowd of enthusiastic fans turned out last Sunday afternoon to see the local team defeat the Battle Lake bunch by a score of 6 to 2. The game was one-sided and uninteresting, Breckenridge having the best of it at all stages. The feature of the game was the batting of Paul Meyers, who in four times up secured a home run, a triple and a double. Thatcher's pitching also came in for a good share of applause, as it was steady, heady and reliable at all times."

In subsequent Battle Lake games, Esten shut down nearby Clitherall on July 11, 9-1, the *Battle Lake Review* described the scene on July 14: "Hansen [sic] pitched for Battle Lake and did well, especially at critical times in the game when there were men on bases."

On July 15, Battle Lake lost to Clitherall, 8-4, and then pitcher Lund helped defeat Deer Creek on July 16, 9-6.

The *Henning Advocate*, on July 27, documented the rematch with Deer Creek, played in neutral Henning, in which Hanson was identified as playing left field, while Lund pitched:

A real game of baseball was played on the local diamond last Sunday between the crack nines of Battle Lake and Deer Creek. It was almost too chilly weather for good playing, but both teams had 'blud' in their eyes, and went at it with a determination to win. Both teams, although neither are as strong as Henning sported last year, are an honor to their respective towns.

That a good game was expected was evidenced by the number of rooters that accompanied each team. Henning people joined in and helped to round out a respectable crowd. Deer Creek went to bat first and scored two tallies. Battle Lake scored one in the third inning, and the score board registered 2 to 1 for several innings. Then Deer Creek made another score and the boys from the lake followed it up and added two more to their lone one, which put the teams on an even footing—3 to 3. The boys continued to white-wash one another until the players resembled white sea gulls. The crowd was getting right into the game. Henning rooters, although supposed to be neutral were inclined to sympathize with the Creekers. There was no change in the standing of the score board at the end of the ninth. At the end of the eleventh inning, Battle Lake, by a heroic effort managed to score and the game was over.

On August 3, the *Henning Advocate* editor, swept up in the quality of play, authored a column comparing that contest to one played in 1891 between Grand Forks, North Dakota, and Fargo, North Dakota, which went twenty-five scoreless innings, with thirty-one men left on base, thirty-seven strikeouts, and ten double plays.

Finally, Battle Lake pummeled Otter Tail City, 10-2, with Esten pitching. Overall, the Battle Lake squad went a respectable 11-4 in 1905, with Esten starting at least six of those games.

Esten had to decide. Already, he knew his father's farm was not large enough to support him and his three unmarried brothers. Playing summer baseball and working side jobs was his only tested alternative. He had proved his mettle on the diamond and had a muscular back to work for others. (The 1905 Minnesota Census of Battle Lake identified him as a "day laborer.") But where would he play baseball and work? In the past, he had followed friends, family, and relatives to play baseball in places such as Minneapolis, Eden Valley, Kerkhoven, and Vining. His brother, Hans, and catcher friend, Charlie Magnuson, had worked in northern lumber camps in the off-season.

In early 1906, *The Banner* reported that Esten's brother, Hans, had married Christine Syverson, and at the wedding the Hanson family had a "jolly good time." The couple went off to live in Churches Ferry, North Dakota. While home for the wedding, Esten no doubt heard of the Kerkhoven baseball team organizing again and of their complete disintegration the year before. He could play for them, but not if they weren't willing to pay him.

If home in February, to earn money, he probably helped his younger brothers chop 1,600 fence posts for their father, and may even have celebrated with them at a dance held in the Sunburg hall later that month. Esten, if present and not being able to hear the music, nevertheless could have felt the vibrations in the floor caused by the dancer's feet as they danced to lively polkas or schottisches, watching them as they whirled around the dance floor. He may have even "tripped the light fantastic" with a young lady of his choice, to the beat and rhythm of a waltz.

Two weeks into the season, the Kerkhoven nine consisted entirely of local boys, and Editor Archer wrote about their victories over Murdock and Willmar Seminary. Once again, not one player, it seemed, was earning money playing baseball for Kerkhoven. The team's pitchers were reported as C. Cottingham, the depot telegrapher, and Ray Cox.

And then suddenly, out of nowhere, *The Banner* reported: "Our boys lost the ball game played here last Sunday with the Benson team by a score of 8 to 6. This was the third game our team played with the Benson boys this season and the county seat team has won every one of them, though in each instance the score has been close enough to make the games interesting. 'Dummy' Hanson, who returned from Canada last week, pitched for the Kerkhoven boys and it seemed quite natural to see him in the game again. Both teams made an abundance of errors in Sunday's game, honors being about even in that respect."

The *Swift County Monitor* describe the game:

The baseball team went down to Kerkhoven Sunday and administered their third defeat to Kerkhoven this season, this time the score standing 6–8. The game was well played and interesting with the exception of loose fielding on the part of Benson's players at critical moments that several time made it appear that Benson's chances look poor, but they managed to come down again after Kerk-hoven tied the score 6-6, and made two more runs, while they held their opponents still. Carl Thronson was on the slab for Benson and pitched his usual good game, while Oscar Arne caught and although he made two errors they are excusable from the fact that he has not had the practice with the team. Hanson, better known as the 'Dummy' fired them for Kerkhoven and while the boys say he has his old time speed he has lost his control, at least for last Sunday, and they found him pretty often for good safe hits.

Esten yielded six runs in eight innings, with five runs coming off him in the first three innings. He struck out six and walked five. Ray Cox came on as a relief pitcher for Esten in the ninth inning, giving up two runs—the deciding two.

Soon thereafter, according to *The Companion*, former student Anthony Lykken reported that Esten had spent the summer playing ball in Estevan, Canada, badly injured his arm after a few games, and returned home. Perhaps Esten was trying to impress Kerkhoven enough to contract his services with them for another year. If he was, he failed miserably. It was his only game pitching for Kerkhoven in 1906.

In 1887, Esten's oldest sister Isabelle married Oliver Thompson of New London, Minnesota. On July 14, 1903, Oliver wrote the *New London Times* to report on his exciting new life in Estevan, Canada, saying, in part, "As most of you are aware, we left our home for this place the 8th of April to take up farming and also to start up the brick yard and coal mine, which is a company organized and incorporated by twelve Kandiyohi Co. [Minnesota] people. I have put in my full time at this point and we have prospered finely."

Perhaps in an effort to quell New London gossipers aware of

his "bad luck" and "sickness" the previous summer, Thompson pointed out that he currently had 100 acres under cultivation, including twenty of flax, and forty of wheat and oats. Apparently his health wasn't all that good. Oliver Thompson's obituary, published in the July 29, 1908, *Willmar Tribune*, mentioned his work as the chief engineer of mines and plants of the Eureka Coal and Brick Company. Given his executive position, and pull with the company, it could be assumed Esten worked there, at least part-time. Any written accounts of Esten's pitching went up in flames though, when the *Estevan Mercury* newspaper building burned years later.

ESTEN'S 1905 BASEBALL SCHEDULE
BATTLE LAKE, MINNESOTA

DATE	OPPONENT	PLAYED AT	WINNER
*May 17	Fergus Falls H. S.	Vining	Vining (?)
May 21	Wadena	Battle Lake	Battle Lake, 7-5
June 4	Breckenridge	Battle Lake	Breckenridge, 5-4
June 16	Vining	Battle Lake	(RAINED OUT)
June 17	Clitherall	Battle Lake	Battle Lake, 7-2
June 18 AM	Wadena	Battle Lake	Battle Lake, 4-3
June 18 PM	Wadena	Battle Lake	Battle Lake, 3-0
June 24	Vining	Battle Lake	Battle Lake, 7-0
June 25	Staples	Battle Lake	Staples, 4-3
July 4	Clitherall	Battle Lake	Battle Lake, 55-10 (?)
July 6	Clitherall	Battle Lake	Battle Lake 4-1
July 9	Breckenridge	Breckenridge	Breckenridge, 6-2
July 11	Clitherall	Clitherall	Battle Lake, 9-1
July 15	Clitherall	Battle Lake	Clitherall, 8-4
July 16	Deer Creek	Battle Lake	Battle Lake, 9-6
July 23	Deer Creek	Henning	Battle Lake, 4-3
July 29	Otter tail	Battle Lake	Battle Lake, 10-2
July 30	Fergus Falls	Battle Lake	(not played)

*NOTE: After joining the Battle Lake "Lakers," Esten made his initial Otter Tail County appearance at the annual Syttende Mai celebration at Vining, Minn.

CHAPTER TWENTY-ONE

McVILLE AND CHAUTAUQUA

In the fall of 1906, Esten migrated to McVille, North Dakota, where his sister, Sarah, and brother, Hans, co-owned a restaurant. Sarah had married Frank Lindberg, and the couple had one son, Everett, born in 1902. Hans, two years older than Sarah, had moved to North Dakota after marrying Christine Syverson.

Verna Johnson Gomer, in a personal interview with this author, revealed that she spoke with the widowed husband, Olney Burtman, of one of Hans' children, Blanche, who confirmed that Sarah and Hans had co-owned a restaurant in McVille, North Dakota, and that Esten had visited it. The *Lakota American* newspaper confirmed this possibility early in August 1906, reporting that, "McVille will have a new restaurant called the Palace." Subsequent news reports proved that Lindberg and Hanson owned the restaurant. McVille was on the verge of becoming a bustling town.

The *McVille Journal* printed its first edition on June 14, and the Great Northern Railroad, expanding to reach McVille grain supplies, reached the town in late September. Speculators moved empty farm buildings into McVille, converted them to storefronts, and built spacious grain elevators. By year's end, the town had a doctor, sidewalks, and about twenty-five businesses, including the two-story Palace Restaurant & Hotel, which served hot and cold lunches. The town also had a baseball team.

After joining his brother and sister that fall, Esten had to endure one of the most severe winters on record. According to Alf Jacobson, a McVille resident formerly of Swift County, in a letter published in *The Banner* on February 9, 1907, the highest temperature in January that year reached ten below, with a recorded low of forty-two below. Jacobson wrote, "The wind is howling in your ears all the time." ·

Waiting patiently for spring, Esten was preparing to play now on his eighth team, which included the Minnesota School for the Deaf nine. R. B. Kilbourn, the town druggist, was chosen as manager. On May 2, 1907, the editor of the *McVille Journal*, L. L. Lang, wrote: "BASE BALL Manager Kilbourn informs the Journal that matters pertaining to base ball are progressing in a favorable manner and the team promises to be a speedy one. The grounds which are located just south of the tracks, are staked out and work will commence as soon as the ground is sufficiently dry. Much interest is being shown by the fans and there is no doubt but that McVille will get its share of the honors in the diamond this year."

The ball team's official sponsor, the McVille Commercial Club, scheduled a basket social for May 10, which was held at the McVille Hotel. The evening's program was rendered by the band and orchestra, raising $142.

Esten, the once-proud pitcher with a rubber-band throwing arm who had faced off against Billy Holland, played catcher most of that summer for McVille. The arm injury from Estevan may have been permanent. Used to being a pitcher, and winning, Esten must have felt awkward playing catcher on a 3-8 squad against teams with unfamiliar names, such as Binford, Lakota, Tolna, Northwood, Hope, and Pekin—not the Atwater, Eden Valley, Clara City, Murdock, and Willmar he had known.

Given McVille's status as a town wet behind the ears, and his position as a catcher, Esten almost certainly didn't earn a salary. The high-octane team up the tracks, Lakota, had the hired guns, not McVille. *McVille Journal* Editor Lang observed, "Lakota is a speedy bunch of salaried players." Lakota beat McVille twice, 8-0 and 13-12.

Esten pitched only once, in a 5-4 loss to Tolna.

Esten, perhaps now believing that his life was in order and his future secured, was thrown a big personal curve ball. He suddenly learned of his father's unexpected death which occurred on July 27, 1907. *The Banner* obituary read:

> Tosten Hanson, one of the pioneer residents of Kerk-
> hoven Township, died at his home in that town last Saturday
> of some liver trouble after an illness of only a few weeks. Up
> to a few weeks ago Mr. Hanson was apparently enjoying
> exceptionally good health for a man of his age and his many
> friends were greatly surprised when they learned of his
> death. Deceased was born in Hallingdal, Norway, Dec. 27,
> 1845, making him a little more than 61 years of age at the

time of his death. With his parents he came to America in the early 50ties. The family first settled in Wisconsin. Later they moved to Rice County, Minn., where they lived for twelve years and then came to Swift County about 35 years ago. Mr. Hanson is survived by his wife and nine children, two sisters, Mrs. Gustave Gysler, of Hamar, Canada, and Mrs. K. O. Lien, of Kerkhoven, and two brothers, Henry and Ole Hanson, of Kerkhoven township.

Immediately after traveling home with relatives to Swift County, and after his father's funeral, Esten did what felt natural, he began playing baseball, only three days after his father's funeral. Apparently, baseball was salve to a wound. Editor Archer announced in *The Banner* in early August, only two weeks after Esten had been identified as playing in McVille, that, "Esten Hanson, who came down from McVille, N. D., last week, has been playing ball with the Kerkhoven team at Spicer this week and pitched one of the games played with the Renville team."

The Kerkhoven boys camped alongside Green Lake in Spicer, and would live there throughout the Chautauqua celebration, August 3–11. In the first game, against New London, in a 5-1 loss, Esten caught Ray Cox, and in the next game, Esten played left field in a 2-1 win against Billy Holland-less Renville. Pitching in his only game of the Chautauqua, Esten lost a 1-0 nail-biter to Renville, striking out four. Esten gave over every ounce of his strength to his pitching, literally. He didn't—or couldn't, due to a sore arm, or wouldn't, because of wanting to be with his family—play in any remaining games of the Chautauqua celebration.

The *Willmar Tribune* recorded Esten's final appearance: "This was a hard fought game all through and was a very clean game of ball, which the score will indicate. Both pitchers pitched a splendid game, Nelson having the best control but 'Dummy' Hanson, the pitcher for Kerkhoven, had good speed and pitched very effective ball, but lost his own game in the first inning by aiding Renville to the only run made in the contest. He gave a base on balls, hit a batter, dropped an infield fly, which filled the bases, and before he could gather himself together he threw the ball to the backstop, allowing a man to score."

Kerkhoven had hired two Minneapolis ballplayers for the Chautauqua celebration, including Jack Phyle, an Indian, who pitched several games. Esten may have wondered if he had a future playing for Kerkhoven, yet his aching right arm could have been confirming otherwise.

Esten stayed home that winter. In March, his heart broke when having to watch his neighbors bid on all his father's farm equipment, and then have a relative, Henry Swenson, rent out their 300 acres to farm. (Betsy would continue living in their new Victorian home until her death in 1923.)

ESTEN'S 1907 BASE BALL SCHEDULE
McVILLE, NORTH DAKOTA

DATE	ESTEN'S POSITION	OPPONENT	WINNER
May 17	Unknown	Aneta	Unknown
May 30?	Unknown	Binford	Binford, 9 to 8
June 13	Catcher	Lakota	Lakota, 8 to 0
June 18	Unknown	Lakota	Lakota 13 0 11
June 21	Pitcher	Tolna	Tolna, 5 to 4
June 23	Catcher	Northwood	McVille, 3 to 1
June 26	Catcher	Tolna	McVille, 2 to 1
July 1	Unknown	Hope	Hope, 10 to 3
July 4	Unknown	Pekin	McVille, 2 to 1
July 18	Unknown	Northwood	Northwood, 1 to 0
			(8 inn.—rain.)

CHAPTER TWENTY-TWO

WHEAT FIELD

With one hand grasping at hope, and the other holding onto home, Esten waited out winter, believing he could play ball for Kerkhoven in 1908. Though thirty, and with an aging arm, he could still pitch effectively at times. Kerkhoven had paid Phyle, why not him? Kerkhoven played its first game of 1908 on May 2 against Willmar Seminary—and with Esten Hanson pitching! He was wearing a green uniform again.

The Banner described the scene:

> The first ball game of the season played here last Saturday afternoon between the Willmar Seminary and Kerkhoven teams, was a close contest and an exciting one. At the end of the 9th inning the score was a tie—4 to 4—and three more innings had to be played before the Kerkhoven players finally scored the winning run. The afternoon was

too cold for the players to do the best work of which they are capable but even so the errors were not so numerous as might have been expected. A fair sized crowd was out to witness the contest.

Esten struck out twelve and allowed only two hits in a 5-4, twelve-inning victory. It would have been natural for Esten to glory in this effort, yet even he, farsighted as he was, could read the writing on the wall. On its roster already, Kerkhoven had two excellent pitchers with spry arms: Ray Cox and seventeen-year-old "Bottle" Berg. The latter was the pitcher of record in Kerkhoven's next game, a ten-strikeout, 15-3 win over DeGraff. Said Editor Archer: "The best feature of the game was the excellent work of the kid battery, Adolph Berg and Clarence Gordhamer. Berg's curves were too much of a puzzle for the DeGraff boys to solve and the hits made off him were few and far between."

Pitchers Cox and Berg finished out the season. In one game, Cox had eighteen strike outs, and in another, Berg, thirteen. Esten's Minnesota pitching career was over, but not his playing career.

When the 1908 Spicer Chautauqua began, New London needed backup position players. The *New London Times* reported: "Esten Hanson of Sunberg was a visitor in our village a few days this week. He accompanied the baseball team to Spicer yesterday and is doing the catching for them during the games with Willmar."

The *Willmar Tribune* summary of the New London-Willmar games mentioned Esten twice: once, for allowing a passed ball, and again, for hitting a double.

By this time, Esten must have realized his hired-gun days as a pitcher were completely over. However, he could still play for the fun of it as long as he was able to throw a baseball. The Kerkhoven baseball season was done, and within a month, he would return to McVille to work, and wait impatiently, for another baseball season.

While in a wheat field, Esten Hanson had an excruciating pain as nothing before, as if his neck and spine had caught fire. We will never be able to fully fathom his state of mind that chaotic morning in September 1908 in northeastern North Dakota.

The *McVille Journal* reported:

Last Sunday evening our city was cast in a deep gloom when it was announced that Esten Hanson was dead. Only a few days ago he left town to work with a threshing crew near Jesse and seemed to be in the best of health. He had only worked a short while when he complained of a head-ache which grew gradually worse until Friday evening when he lapsed into unconsciousness from which he never rallied. His relatives who reside in this city were notified and he was brought to town Saturday. Everything possible was done for the young man by a skilled physician and faithful friends, but he gradually sank until the hand of death relieved him of his suffering at 10:30 Sunday evening. The immediate cause of death was acute meningitis. Esten Hanson was born about thirty-one years ago near Kerkhoven, Minn., where he spent the greater part of his life. He was unfortu-nate in that he was born a deaf mute, but he was also fortunate to have parents who gave him every possible advantage to overcome the handicap by giving him a liberal education. He graduated several years ago from the

Faribault school for the deaf, where he also learned the printer's trade. Poor eyesight prevented him from following the trade of a printer steadily but at times he would hold a case when his eyes would permit. At one time he assisted in the Journal shop and was very efficient. He first came to this city about a year and a half ago, since which time he has made his home with Mr. and Mrs. F. A. Lindberg, Mrs. Lindberg being his sister. During his residence here he made many friends, who sincerely regret his untimely demise. Deceased leaves a mother, five sisters and three brothers to mourn the loss of a kind son and loving brother. The remains were taken to the old home at Kerkhoven where interment was made.

The Banner described the scene:

Esten, better known as Dummy Hanson, a son of Mrs. T. Hanson, of Monson lake, died at McVille, N. Dak., September 20 of brain fever. The remains were shipped back here and interred in the Monson Lake cemetery on Wednesday last week. He was about 28 years of age. Deceased is the young man who a few years ago gained considerable distinction in this part of the state as a baseball player, being the pitcher for the Kerkhoven team. He was deaf and dumb but this affliction he bore cheerfully and was at all times in the best of spirits. In a ball game he was a most enthusiastic player and a favorite with the fans and his team mates."

Upon request of Dr. Tate of the Minnesota School for the Deaf, the following news item appeared in *The Companion* on October 7, 1908:

A few days ago Dr. Tate received a letter from Mrs. T. Hanson of Kerkhoven, Minn., informing him of the death of her son Esten, Sept. 20, from an attack of brain fever. His death occurred at his sister's home, at McVille, N. D., after an illness of only three days. He was 31 years old and left school ten years ago. Esten was a good boy at school, studious and obedient. But he will be best remembered by his schoolmates for his skill as a baseball pitcher. He seemed to have a natural talent for pitching, and did fine work for the team. After leaving school he often played with hearing baseball teams during the summer, and was probably one of the best amateur pitchers in the state. We are sorry to hear of his death in the prime of life, and we extend our sympathy to his bereaved relatives.

BIBLIOGRAPHY

PUBLICATIONS

Anonsen, Stanley Holte. *A History of Swift County.* Appleton, MN: Appleton Press, 1929.

Community Fact Survey. McVille, North Dakota. 1966.

Crosby, Frank. *Everybody's Lawyer and Counselor In Business.* Philadelphia: John E. Potter, 1860.

History Book Committee of the McVille (ND) Centennial Committee. *McVille: The First 100 Years.* 2006.

Hoffbeck, Steven R. *Swinging for the Fences: Black Baseball in Minnesota.* Minnesota Historical Society Press, 2005.

Lane, Harlan, Robert Hoffmeister, and Ben Bahan. *A Journey into the Deaf-World.* San Diego: DawnSignPress, 1996.

Lauritsen, Wesley, L.H.D. *Minnesota School for the Deaf 1863–1963.* Faribault, MN: 1963.

McVille Golden Jubilee, June 25–26–27, 1956. McVille, ND: McVille Golden Jubilee Committee, 1956.

McVille North Dakota, 1906–1981. McVille 75th Committee: 1981.

Solyst, E.W., and Gladys. *A Century of Progress.* Warren, MN: Warren Sheaf, Neal Mattson, 1981.

Swift County Historical Society. *Images of America, Swift County, Minnesota.* Benson, MN: Swift County Historical Society, 2000.

The Elks Family Resource Center. *My Turn to Learn.* Surrey, B.C.: Elks Family Resource Center, 1997.

Wendland, Audrey Kvam. *The Hanson Family.* Niceville, FL: Printing Press of Niceville, 1996.

DOCUMENTS

Minnesota Institution for the Education of the Deaf and Dumb (Faribault, MN). *Annual Report to the Legislature and Governor of the State of Minnesota (1863–1865).* 1889.

Minnesota Institute for Defectives (Faribault, MN). *Biennial Report to the Governor of Minnesota (1889–1899).*

Norway Lake Parish (New London, MN). *Birth and Marriage Records.* 1861–1890.

North Dakota Department of Health, Division of Vital Records (Bismarck, ND).

State Historical Society of North Dakota (Bismark, ND).

State of Minnesota and U.S. Census. 1870–1905 (excluding 1890 U.S. Census [destroyed by fire]).

PERIODICALS

Alexandria (MN) Republican

Aneta (ND) Panorama

Atwater Republican (MN) Press

Battle Lake (MN) Review

Benson (MN) Times

Chippewa County (Clara City, MN) Herald

Chippewa County (Clara City, MN) Journal

Dassel (MN) Anchor

Estevan (Saskatchewan, Canada) Mercury

Faribault (MN) Democrat, The

Faribault (MN) Republican, The

Fergus Falls (MN) Weekly Journal, The

Glenwood (MN) Herald

Glenwood (MN) Messenger

Henning (MN) Advocate

Kandiyohi County (Willmar, MN) Expositor

Kerkhoven (MN) Standard

Kerkhoven (MN) Banner, The

Lakota (ND) American, The

McVille (ND) Journal

Minnesota State Academy for the Deaf (Faribault, MN) Companion

Minnesota State Academy for the Deaf (Faribault, MN) Mute's Companion

Montevideo (MN) Commercial

Morris (MN) Sun, The

Morris (MN) Times

Morris (MN) Tribune, The

Murdock (MN) Messenger

Murdock (MN) Voice

New London (MN) Review

New London (MN) Times

Paynesville (MN) Press, The

Raymond (MN) News

Renville (MN) Star Farmer

Swift County (Benson, MN) Advocate

Swift County (Benson, MN) Monitor

Swift County (Benson, MN) Review

Swift County (Kerkhoven, MN) Standard, The

Wilkin County (Breckenridge, MN) Gazette

Willmar (MN) Republican Gazette

Willmar (MN) Tribune, The

PERSONAL LETTERS to the AUTHOR

Gomer, Verna Johnson. Glenwood, MN.

Gordhamer, Myrtice. Alexandria, MN.

Nelson, Vivian Hanson. Grove City, MN.

Wendland, Audrey Kvam. Niceville, FL.

PERSONAL INTERVIEWS with the AUTHOR

Cashman, Michael (Newark, DE, teacher, Delaware School for the Deaf; graduate of MSAD and Gallaudet University, Washington, DC, baseball player).

Gomer, Verna Johnson (Glenwood, MN, Esten Hanson's niece), first interview in May 2002.

Johnson, Henry (Kerkhoven, MN, author's grandfather), mid-1930s.

Mathews, John (Faribault, MN, MSAD graduate), November 2002.

Nelson, Vivian Hanson (Grove City, MN, Esten Hanson's niece), May 2002.

Olson, David (MSAD graduate and athletic director), June 2002.

Potter, Jim (Faribault, MN, MSAD graduate), November 2002.

Rood, Elmo, and Mary Rood (Sunburg, MN, present owners of Esten Hanson's farm home), Summer 2002.

Present faculty, administration, and students of MSAD (Faribault, MN), 2003–2008.

Recent MSAD graduate (Faribault MN), November 2002.

BACKGROUND RESOURCES

Bio-Medical Research Library, University of Minnesota, Minneapolis, MN.

Kandiyohi County Historical Society, Willmar, MN.

Minnesota Historical Society, St. Paul, MN.

National Baseball Hall of Fame and Museum, Cooperstown, NY.

North Dakota Funeral Directors Association, Grafton, ND.

Pope County Historical Society, Glenwood, MN.

Rice County Historical Society, Faribault, MN.

State Historical Society of North Dakota, Bismarck, ND.

Swift County Historical Society, Benson, MN.

Owen H. Wangensteen Historical Library of Biology and Medicine, University of Minnesota, Minneapolis, MN.

City Auditor's Office, McVille, ND.

Oregon Area Historical Museum, Oregon, WI.

PHOTOGRAPHS

Gordhamer, Mr. and Mrs. Robert, Alexandria, MN.

Gomer, Verna Johnson. Glenwood, MN.

Johnson, Jim.

Minnesota Historical Society. St. Paul, MN.

Paulson, Florice. Oregon, WI.

WEB SITES

National Italian American Sports Hall of Fame, www.niashf.org.

Vintage Base Ball Association (Ladies Vintage Base Ball), http://wiki.vbba.org.

ABOUT THE AUTHOR

Jim Johnson, a native of Kerkhoven, Minnesota, experienced sandlot, American Junior Legion, and town team baseball.

Graduating from Concordia College (Moorhead, Minnesota) in 1954, he taught high school history and coached athletics at Elbow Lake, Minnesota.

After receiving his Juris Doctor from the William Mitchell College of Law (St. Paul, Minnesota) in 1961, he practiced law in St. Cloud, Minnesota, and in Benson, Minnesota, during which time he was also elected to the office of Swift County Attorney.

Jim is a member of the Halsey Hall Chapter of The Society for American Baseball Research and is a contributing columnist for *The Kerkhoven Banner*.

Retired, he and his wife, parents of two daughters, live in Minneapolis.